The
Tsardom
of
Muscovy

Alexander E. Presniakov

The Tsardom of
Muscovy

EDITED AND TRANSLATED BY

ROBERT F. PRICE

❧❧❧❧❧❧❧❧❧❧❧❧❧❧❧❧❧❧

WITH

Master and Man in Muscovy

BY

Charles J. Halperin

❧❧❧❧❧❧❧❧❧❧❧❧❧❧❧❧❧❧

Academic International Press: 1986

THE RUSSIAN SERIES / Volume 30

Alexander E. Presniakov, *The Tsardom of Muscovy*.
Translation of *Moskovskoe tsarstvo* (Petrograd,
1918).

Library of Congress Catalog Card Number: 77-78432
ISBN: 0-87569-090-4 (paper edition)

Composition by Jeanette Rawlinson and Jean MacNeil
Title page by King & Queen Press

Printed in the United States of America

*A list of Academic International Press publications
is found at the end of this volume.*

ACADEMIC INTERNATIONAL PRESS
Box 1111 Gulf Breeze FL 32561

CONTENTS

CONTENTS

MASTER AND MAN IN MUSCOVY

Historians devote a great deal of time and energy to the problem of periodization, and scholars in Russian history are no exception. The adoption of Christianity by Saint Vladimir in 988, the Mongol conquest of the thirteenth century, the Time of Troubles at the turn of the seventeenth century, the reforms of Peter the Great at the turn of the eighteenth century, the Great Reforms of Alexander II of the nineteenth century, the Russian Revolutions of 1905 and 1917—Russian history is constantly punctuated with dramatic and often violent interruptions, whose causes and consequences for the development of Russia remain matters of tremendous dispute. The relationship between the first period of East Slavic history, that of the Kievan state of the ninth-twelfth centuries, and the Muscovite state of the sixteenth and seventeenth centuries, also has aroused considerable attention, at least in part because of the intrusion of ethnic biases. Yet common sense suggests that in the seemless web of history, in any century there are elements of continuity and discontinuity. The task of the historian is not merely to repeat this self-evident point, but rather to go beyond vague and dogmatic generalizations to identify precisely the elements of the old and the new in a given historical epoch. His challenge is to analyze the processes at work which resulted in the formation of the newer state and society. To accomplish this goal objectively and convincingly requires, to be sure, considerable skill.

It is difficult to imagine a more successful exercise of just such skill than A.E. Presniakov's *The Tsardom of Muscovy*.*

*This essay is much indebted to the "Introduction" by Alfred J. Rieber

Presniakov was one of the most brilliant scholars of the late nineteenth and early twentieth centuries to devote himself to the study of medieval Russia. He possessed an enormous familiarity with the primary sources of early Russian history and an unflagging respect for their integrity. Therefore he approached the sources without any preconceptions. He eschewed the broad conceptual schemes of his famous predecessors, Soloviev and Kliuchevsky, for example, for the meticulous investigation of specific historical problems. His numerous monographs demonstrate an abiding scepticism toward the grand pictures then and even now current about Russian history. For this reason Presniakov's total work contains a profound reappraisal of almost all of early Russian history and constitutes a scholarly contribution easily the equal of any of his precursors. In addition Presniakov eagerly learned from a diversity of nascent intellectual disciplines ranging from social psychology to ethnography. In particular he studied the works of the great linguist A.A. Shakhmatov, who was then inventing Old Russian textology, the analysis of manuscripts and texts from a rigorously philological standpoint.

Presniakov shied away from flashy conclusions. In general his work is not noted for powerful synthesis or comprehensive summary. On the other hand, Presniakov remains a past and unexcelled master in the field of political history, where his method permitted him to demolish previous generalizations by demonstrating the complexity, irregularity, even sheer perversity of the course of human events, which refuse to arrange themselves neatly and rationally solely for the benefit of the historian. In Presniakov attention to narrative detail in political history became an imaginative conceptual tool. Nowhere is this better illustrated than in his classic study of the political history of northeast Russia during the thirteenth to fifteenth

to A.E. Presniakov, *The Formation of the Great Russian State*, tr. A.E. Moorhouse (Chicago, 1970), pp. xxi-xlii, and to the several as yet unpublished studies by James C. Mills, "Presniakov in Two Worlds: A 'Bourgeois Historian' and the Soviet Revolution" and "The Russian Autocracy in the Writings of A.E. Presniakov," whom I wish to thank for copies of his papers.

centuries, *The Formation of the Great Russian State*. Indeed, most subsequent investigations of this period are no more than commentaries on Presniakov's great monograph.

The Tsardom of Muscovy, by contrast, has something very different to offer. This is the closest Presniakov ever came to writing genuine synthesis. In this extended narrative essay he attempted to summarize and analyze the evolution of the Muscovite state and society from the middle of the fifteenth to the seventeenth centuries. It is hardly surprising that Presniakov drew on earlier works of other scholars, some of which he identifies and more of which will be obvious to specialists. Further research has modified some of his conclusions, but Presniakov's overall analysis could hardly be called controversial any more, and he is far more right than wrong. Yet as a work of synthesis *The Tsardom of Muscovy* is deceptive, because its admirably laconic prose contains a startlingly complex and original argument about the shuffling and reshuffling of social and political elements which transpired during the sixteenth and seventeenth centuries, and about the role, function and evolution of the new monarchy of Muscovy in Russian history. Presniakov's study, intended for a more general audience than most of his previous publications, stands out as a major achievement in historical judgment. In its coherence and logic it remains the most stimulating and convincing overview of Muscovy available.

Presniakov traces the antecedents of early modern Muscovy to the twelfth century northeast Russia of Vladimir and Suzdal, to the era of its great builders, Yury Dolguruky, Andrei Bogoliubsky, and Vsevolod "Big Nest." It is not just that the Muscovites themselves later propagated a view of Muscovy as the successor and legitimate heir of Suzdalia. Presniakov also argues that there was a real and identifiable link between fifteenth-century Muscovy and twelfth-century Suzdalia—the exigencies of geography and geopolitics. Both states were located in the Volga-Oka river mesopotamia, and Presniakov proposes that any such state would face the problem of mobilizing sufficient economic and military resources for defense. It would likewise have pretensions to control the natural trade outlets to the Baltic in the great port of Novgorod and down the Volga to the rich market of Persia and the world of Islam. The connection between a Bogoliubsky and an Ivan the Terrible does not lie solely in the ideological sphere of the doctrine of autocracy. It can be found in foreign policies rooted in physical necessity; as the former moved against the Volga Bulgars so the latter conquered the Tatar khanates of Kazan and Astrakhan.

Presniakov sees an organic relationship between the grand principality of Moscow of the fourteenth and early fifteenth century and the later tsardom of Muscovy of the sixteenth and seventeenth centuries, which is often overlooked. The historical processes which permitted and even compelled Moscow to play the role of unifier of the Great Russian people created the framework within which the development of the autocracy of the Muscovite tsardom was certainly a foregone conclusion, if not a virtual necessity. Northeast Russia suffered from chronic underpopulation and relatively primitive economic and technological development. Its unification required the centralization of authority and power within the governmental apparatus. The natural outgrowth of the "gathering of the Russian lands" by the "patrimonial *principality*" of Moscow, itself an imitation of twelfth century Suzdalia, was the "patrimonial *autocracy*" of Moscow.

An historical axiom states that quantitative change produces qualitative change. The Muscovy which sprang from the unification process could not respond to the political situation of the sixteenth century without changing itself via reform. Presniakov presents a sensitive portrait of the steps taken by the Muscovite government to mobilize, indeed sometimes to create, the huge human and financial resources required to address the problems imposed on it. The earlier Muscovite principality had neither displayed nor desired the ability to administer directly its growing territory. The social, political and military base of the regime was the boyar aristocracy. The boyars in effect governed their patrimonial estates in the interests of the state. They also comprised its administrative elite. Yet the system of governors and reliance upon the traditional power of the aristocracy would not now suffice in the tsardom of Muscovy. Beginning with the reign of Ivan III the Great (1462-1503), therefore, the regime embarked upon a policy of massive, centrally-directed social change, a policy still not fully appreciated, let alone understood by scholars. The state essentially created a new class, the gentry or *dvoriane*, who were given conditional land grants or *pomestie*-fiefs in return for military service. The gentry class was designed to constitute a new social base upon which the autocracy could rely for support against the conservative aristocracy. They could supply the additional civilian and military officials without whom the ambitious domestic and foreign policies of the regime could not succeed.

According to Presniakov, the Muscovite aristocracy believed that the traditional ways of doing things, which they called custom, were the best, and should not be changed. The boyars, especially those of princely origin, therefore resisted the increasing accumulation of power in the hands of the ruler, the autocrat, in the sixteenth century. Yet, Presniakov argues, the autocrat had to break the bonds of tradition if the Muscovite government were to meet its obligations at home and abroad. The contradiction between an autocratic, reform-minded monarchy and an administration run by conservative aristocrats devoted to their own class privileges and to an older way of life, could not endure.

The most violent explosion to result from this contradiction came during the reign of Ivan IV the Terrible (1530-1585). Ivan established the oprichnina as a private domain where his bodyguards and troops had unlimited power. He launched a reign of terror against the aristocracy. He sought by executions and deportations to destroy their patrimonial landholding base and break the back of their opposition to his rule.

Although this interpretation is still widespread, it can also be questioned. Boyars had been prominent in the enactment of the reforms of the first part of Ivan's reign, before the establishment of the oprichnina in 1564, and the reforms themselves were not directed against the boyar class. Boyars served in the oprichnina, and continued to occupy the highest positions and offices in the army and the civil administration. A majority of the victims of the oprichnina were not even members of the aristocracy. An alternative explanation of the oprichnina must be sought.

Presniakov refers to Ivan the Terrible's well-known paranoia, arbitrariness, and cruel excesses. Yet he does not, wisely I think, endorse the view, also still maintained, that Ivan was psychotic and that his personality "explains" his sadistic actions, such as the oprichnina. I would go even further in rejecting this view, because there is no way to understand how a madman could continue to run an effective foreign policy until his death, or why anyone in Muscovy so blithely obeyed his decrees.

Presniakov presents in passing an alternative and sophisticated resolution of the problem of Ivan the Terrible. Ivan's behavior, including his sadism and paranoia, reflects the depths of the crisis which Muscovy already faced. The extremism of Ivan's actions personifies the anguish and social anxiety caused by the distance between what the state demanded of the population and what the people could actually provide. Although this observation is not developed by Presniakov and it cannot explain the precise symbolism of Ivan's acts, nevertheless it is an intriguing and convincing insight.

Presniakov shows that the aristocracy as a whole did not oppose the doctrines of autocracy, despite their adherence to custom. Prince Andrei Kurbsky, who exchanged polemical letters with his former sovereign after defecting to Poland during the Livonian War, argued not for a "constitutional" regime but for a more enlightened autocracy, one in which Ivan IV would pay greater attention to his "wise advisors." Certainly the aristocrats did want greater security of person and property. They sought to achieve these things during the reign of the boyar tsar, Vasily Shuisky (1606-1608), and in their negotiations with the king of Poland in 1610. However, in the long run these attempts were unsuccessful.

Even in the sixteenth century the boyars were caught between two inconsistent desires. They wanted the regularity of law and inviolability of person and property—which meant boyar privilege—that would have come with a "state of law" or *Rechtsstaat*. They also wished for a personal, absolute and philanthropic ruler who could protect them from injustice and reward them individually with great office and careers. Much eighteenth century Russian history reflects this basic ambivalence of the Russian elite toward autocracy. It provides useful insights into sixteenth century developments as well, I would contend.

I would propose that the Muscovite autocracy sought to refashion the aristocracy to meet its new needs and demands. Diluting its monopoly of office and power by creating new military servitors in the gentry and new civil officials in the *diaki*, to whom I will return, did not mean completely displacing the boyars as a class. The goal was to render the aristocracy more responsive and pliant. Many boyars served the new autocracy loyally. I am struck by the analogy to the problem of the relationship of the aristocracy to Peter the Great, who "westernized" the aristocracy while conserving its social and political exclusivity. In the sixteenth century the aristocracy never rejected the development of autocracy, and Presniakov describes how the regime sought to mobilize the aristocracy on its own terms. Unfortunately, I think, he did not completely confront the implications of such a view for the usual presentation of Ivan the Terrible's reign.

Presniakov devotes the most space to the two most important groups in society, the land-owning classes of the aristocracy and gentry. He also discusses somewhat more briefly other elements of society—the peasantry, the merchants and artisans, the clergy and the civil officials. Presniakov argues that in the sixteenth and seventeenth centuries the Muscovite state subordinated *all* classes to its own needs, mobilized all segments of Muscovite society to increase their contributions in service and taxes to the regime. Just as the autocracy manipulated the gentry and the aristocracy, so did it impose itself upon other social groups as well. This concept is an original and seminal generalization in approaching Muscovite and Russian history, and forms the *leitmotif* of *The Tsardom of Muscovy*. Let's look at Presniakov's comments on each of these classes.

The new gentry were totally dependent upon the state for their fiefs, and the regime used them in the vastly expanded army and governmental institutions. The peasants had been largely free personally and self-governing. The state had to guarantee to the gentry a docile and stable labor force, without which grants of land would be worthless. Therefore the government pursued a policy of enserfment, of binding the peasants to the land and inhibiting their free movement. The peasants bitterly resented this diminution of their accustomed rights, and appealed to the tsar for redress of grievances. The tsar turned a deaf ear to their petitions. The security of the state rested on the economic and social superiority of the gentry and aristocracy, whose interests the autocrat served above all else. The state also froze the tax-paying artisans in their suburbs to provide a consistent source of revenue.

Presniakov shows how the state coopted the leading merchants into the guild of wealthy merchants (*gosti*) to serve as commercial agents of the government and as tax collectors. He offers some suggestive and on the whole cogent reasons for the lack of opposition by the church to the development of autocracy.

I would contend, however, that Presniakov did not throw his net widely enough in looking at the social changes in sixteenth-century Muscovy produced by the new restructuring of society. Of course, one can excuse his brevity for lack of space in a short essay. But the social crisis of Muscovy which was produced by the very processes of social mobilization he so perceptively emphasizes was then exacerbated by the Livonian War (1558-1583) and the dislocations of the oprichnina. Eventually it exploded in the anarchy and chaos of the Time of Troubles (1598-1613), when Muscovite state and society disintegrated and Muscovy was nearly conquered by Poland. I think there is much more to be said than Presniakov hints.

Presniakov does not mention the evidence of reform of the clergy provided by sixteenth century monastic rules and regulations or by the decisions of the ecclesiastical council of one-hundred chapters (*Stoglav*) of 1550. These sought to raise the level of the clergy and make liturgical practices uniform in Muscovy. He does not allude to the indications of religious unrest in the form of heretical groups of the middle of the sixteenth century, whose "free-thinking" is much akin to certain Protestant sects. He does not mention very clearly the creation of a new group of semi-professional, semi-artisanal infantry, the musketeers (*streltsy*), who later caused Peter the Great so much trouble.

Uncited is the first Muscovite book of household management, the *Domostroi*. This book instructs its regrettably unknown readership in how to run a virtually capitalistic household. It emphasizes the virtues of thrift, frugality, and bargain-hunting, to say nothing of the economic benefits of close supervision of servants. In religious matters its preference is for formalism and propriety, ethical and discrete behavior, rather than the asceticism or mysticism often found in the Russian religious tradition. Certainly philanthropy and charity would not have come easy to someone following its precepts. The fear of engaging in conspicuous consumption might reflect the insecurities and anxieties of newer social groups in society. On the whole the *Domostroi* embodies to me a resoundingly bourgeois and Puritan ethos, whose very appearance in sixteenth century Muscovy requires further study. Identical tensions about social mobility and status must lie at the base of the flowering of legislation on "injured honor" (*bezchestie*) in the *Sudebnik* (law code) of 1550, which penalized insults to individuals according to their new social standings.

The overwhelming need to maintain social control and stability in an age of profound social change is manifested in the ever-widening application of the principle of "collective responsibility" (*krugovaia poruka*) and the duty to denounce to the authorities any anti-social, especially treasonous, activity. Presniakov only mentions in passing legislation to eliminate brigandage (the *guba* reform). This measure established a very harsh and drastic machinery to catch and punish, often with the death penalty, all criminals. It demonstrates the heightened ambitiousness of the bureaucracy to restore law and order as well as its confidence that it had the ability to do so. Its urgency suggests too the dangerousness of the problem, as displaced or unsuccessful members of all social classes turned to lives of crime in desperation at the multiplying demands of the regime upon society.

Presniakov is too cautious, I believe, in relegating the development of the Muscovite bureaucracy to the seventeenth century. The departments (*prikazi*) and crown secretaries (*diaki*) arose in the sixteenth century. The obsessive concern with rigorously prescribed legal procedures in Muscovite law codes and edicts surely testifies to the ethos of a growing bureaucratic social group of literate, professional civil servants. Even by the end of the fifteenth century we know that court cases were decided upon the basis of the written and oral evidence presented. The crown secretaries served as a counterweight to the boyar ascendency in the apparatus of government. Like the gentry, the *diaki* depended upon the state for their existence. Their service mentality, similar to that of the gentry, derived from that dependence, although the crown secretaries occupied important positions of influence within the governmental administration.

The need for a social outlet for the tension produced on every class of Muscovite society by this vast social transformation might explain the growing xenophobia of Muscovite society. This animosity toward those who spoke a different language or professed a different religion became endemic in Russia after the Time of Troubles. Under Metropolitan Makary in the middle of the sixteenth century new levels of anti-Islamic fanaticism were reached, foreshadowing forced conversions and religious unrest in the future by Muscovy's Muslim subjects. Worse yet was the emerging and more highly articulated anti-Jewish prejudice which generated a policy of conscious exclusion of all Jews from Muscovy. Ivan IV wrote the king of Poland that all his merchants were welcome in Muscovy except Jews. When Muscovite armies conquered the city of Polotsk in the Livonian War the Jewish population was massacred.

Finally, Presniakov slights the intellectual area. A new political theory arose in Russia in the sixteenth century declaring the necessity for rule by terror to maintain order. It is very reminiscent of Machiavelli's ideas on whether a ruler should be loved or feared. This ideology expressed the general malaise and unease produced by the attempt of the state to mobilize human and financial resources to meet external needs beyond the ability of society to bear. The consequence of the disparity between what the autocracy demanded and Muscovite society could provide was the catastrophic collapse of all social and political institutions during the Troubles, when the Muscovite masses gave vent to their hatred of the gentry in a general uprising.

In his firm statement of the general outline of the social change in sixteenth-century Muscovy, Presniakov took a great step forward. He possessed a broad-ranging familiarity with European history, but he lacked the willingness to see the evolution of Muscovy in a comparative perspective. Presniakov does comment on the superficial similarities and to him more serious dissimilarities between the "councils of the land" (*zemskie sobory*) and the various estates-general of Western Europe. He does make some tantalizing references to how Russia skipped the phase of "gentry monarchy" of (mostly Eastern) Europe. But he does not recognize the structural and social parallels between the creation of a bureaucratized, centralized and gradually secularized state in Muscovy and the similar processes of the rise of the so-called "new monarchies" in Western Europe in the early modern period. Presniakov underlined the crucial importance of Russia's entrance into the European state system for its domestic evolution. He did not pursue any possible analogies to that evolution of Muscovy to generally similar developments in, say, England, France, Spain and Prussia. While the differences between Russia and the rest of Europe usually draw the most attention, the congruence of Muscovite social evolution to that of much of Europe remains clouded. For example, it is curious that the gentries of Poland, Bohemia and Hungary achieved the enserfment of their peasantries via the creation of gentry, "constitutional" monarchies, while in Muscovy the development of enserfment and autocracy proceeded in tandem. Aristocratic emigres across the Polish-Muscovite border in the sixteenth century did not find their social status imperilled by differing cultural and political practices. I think that more flexible comparative analysis of sixteenth-century Muscovy and the rest of Europe will improve considerably our understanding of Muscovite society. Something other than the notion of "backwardness" is needed to comprehend how the early modern Muscovite state was built using political methods, such as the fief, long out of use in Western Europe.

Presniakov makes the original suggestion that the Time of Troubles, usually seen as the nadir of autocratic authority, actually contributed to the development of autocracy. The two classes most responsible for the restoration of order, the gentry and the traders and artisans, actively sought the restitution of centralized monarchical authority after the Troubles as a reaction to the unrest of civil war of that era. No doubt the bureaucracy also shared these sentiments.

Presniakov's analysis of the history of the seventeenth century is fairly traditional. The power of the autocracy continued to grow, and neither the gentry nor the aristocracy seriously opposed it. In part this political passivity resulted from the shrewdness of the regime in satisfying the major demand of its servitor class, the gentry, in the definitive enserfment of the Russian peasantry accomplished in the Law Code (*Ulozhenie*) of 1649. At the same time, the tax-free enclaves of artisans belonging to monasteries or boyars were abolished, and the entire artisanal population transformed into a closed caste.

I don't think anyone would disagree that the enserfment of the peasantry represented the autocracy's recognition of the social and political importance of the gentry. Still, the dominance of the gentry cannot constitute a total explanation of the process. The government was surprisingly slow to meet this essential demand of its army. This reluctance to proceed to enserfment must derive either from the selfishness of a small circle of court favorites who were stealing peasants from the gentry, or from the refusal of the bureaucracy to burden itself further with law suits for the recovery of runaways once the statute of limitations were repealed. Most likely both must be taken into account.

Presniakov proposes with justification that the need to recover territory lost during the Troubles and to rebuild the economic and social structure of Muscovy required increased reliance by the autocracy upon its bureaucratic administration. Continued efforts to reform the state apparatus sought to minimize corruption and maximize efficiency in the desire to generate yet more resources to meet the insatiable demands of the state.

Yet the recreation of the social and political system of the sixteenth century would not have satisfied the needs of the Great Russian state of the seventeenth century, even once the losses of the Troubles were made good. Presniakov refers to further changes in Muscovy in addition to enserfment. Secularization of the state produced the subordination of the Church and Tsar Alexis's triumph over Patriarch Nikon. Muscovy turned toward Western Europe as a source of expertise—military, technological, and cultural. These are all well-known features of the seventeenth century, which is traditionally seen as a period of "transition" in Muscovite history. This is Presniakov's view as well. With the acquisition of the Ukraine and Siberia, Muscovy broke out of the geographic region of northeast Russia and the ethnic limits of the Great Russians. In so doing it started down the path to its transformation into the multi-ethnic and "enlightened" Russian Empire of Peter the Great and the eighteenth century. Presniakov effectively invokes the critique of·the Croat immigrant Krizhanich of the "old" Russia to dramatize the birth-pangs of the "new" Russia to come, and on this note he concludes his study of the Muscovite tsardom.

In *The Tsardom of Muscovy* Presniakov tried to telescope the development of Muscovite autocracy in its relationship to Muscovite society and institutions over some two hundred very involved years of history. To reduce the uneven and tortuous developments of this period to a reasonable compass is an ambitious goal. To present the wealth of detail necessary to flesh out generalizations without overwhelming the reader in a mass of incoherent facts is a formidable task. It is to Presniakov's credit that he succeeded in doing these things without sacrificing either the complexity or the logic of the course of

events. Presniakov avoided both distortion and unjustified cli-
ches. *The Tsardom of Muscovy* is a classic of its kind.

Presniakov observes that the ideology of the Russian autocracy of the nineteenth century had its roots in Muscovite times.
It is not surprising that Presniakov went on to write several
studies of Imperial Russian history in a format similar to *The
Tsardom of Muscovy*. His scholarly reputation, however, rests
primarily on his work as a medievalist. It is to be celebrated
that his ideas about the Muscovite state now will be accessible
to interested readers not familiar with the Russian language
through this fine translation.

Charles J. Halperin

Indiana University

INTRODUCTION

In 1487, at the Reichstag in Nuremburg, Emperor Friedrich III and princes of the Holy Roman Empire listened with amazement as the knight Nicholas Poppel told of distant Muscovy. Due to his involvement in the extensive dynastic politics of the Jagellonian princes of Poland,[1] the emperor was greatly interested in the affairs of Eastern Europe. It was a pleasant surprise for him to learn of the existence of a powerful, independent Eastern state which was opposed to the Polish-Lithuanian Commonwealth.[2] Poppel later returned to Moscow, at the beginning of 1489, as the imperial ambassador with the mission of bending Muscovite policy to suit Habsburg interests. His task was to propose family bonds to Grand Prince Ivan III Vasilievich[3] in the form of a marriage of Ivan's daughter to the emperor's nephew Albrecht, Margrave of Baden. Furthermore, the grand principality of Moscow would be brought into the Holy Roman Empire by endowing the grand prince with the title of king.

The Habsburg ambassador was surprised when these proposals did not tempt the northern ruler. The prince of Muscovy gave an unexpected, haughty reply. In the name of Grand Prince Ivan, Poppel was informed, "By God's grace we have been rulers of our land since the beginning, from our earliest forebears. Just as our ancestors, we have been appointed by God, and we ask God that we as well as our children may be allowed to rule as heretofore. As we have not previously desired other appointments from anyone, so now we do not want them."

The Greek George Trachaniot,[4] in a return mission the same year from the grand prince to the emperor in Frankfurt, further replied that it was not proper for a grand prince to give his daughter in marriage to a margrave. The grand prince traced his heritage to Byzantium; he ruled many lands, and from early times his predecessors had been friends and brothers to Holy

Roman emperors who had relinquished Rome to the pope. Moscow, therefore, would consider only the imperial heir apparent, Maximilian, as a suitable match for the daughter of the grand prince. Thus for the first time Western diplomacy observed a new political force in Eastern European affairs, and one which could not be ignored. Furthermore, Moscow took its place in full awareness of its independence and special interests.

This was a novel development not only for the imperial Reichstag, but for the government of the Empire as well. The last decades of the fifteenth century witnessed events of the greatest historical significance in Eastern Europe. It was a time of fundamental reorientation of all political forces in the region. Moscow was completing the long task of unifying the Great Russian state. Only six years before Poppel's initial visit to Russia, Moscow had emerged from vassalage to the khans of the Golden Horde[5] to become an autocratic (in the original sense), sovereign state.

Eight years had passed since Grand Prince Ivan III had subjugated Novgorod the Great,[6] and Moscow had taken control of that city's Western connections and relations. Moscow had become involved in the struggle to master the Baltic sea, seeking an alliance with Denmark to protect a free sea route from west to east. The Swedes sought to dominate all passage on the Baltic. The grand prince was the natural enemy of the Polish-Lithuanian Jagellonian rulers as they vied for control of Western Russian territories. He exercised a threatening restraint on the Jagellonian dynastic policy of acquiring the Czech and Hungarian crowns which were also being sought by the Habsburgs. In southern affairs—the fall of the Golden Horde and the beginning of the protracted struggle of the Muscovite state with the Tatar world—Moscow's interests coincided with the beloved dreams of Western politicians of an attack by Christian Europe against the Moslem East to expel the Turk from the Balkan peninsula.

The tale that the knight Poppel told of the unknown land of Muscovy contains some naive rhetoric. The West already knew about Muscovy without him, about its rapid advances and the link of Muscovite affairs with relationships on the Baltic and Black seas. It was here, to the distant North, that the Greeks and the Balkan Slavs had looked with premature hope of active aid, disappointed in their expectations of Western European support. Here, even as early as the 1470s, the Venetian senate had turned with declarations concerning the rights of the Muscovite sovereign to the Byzantine heritage.[7] Venice was assessing the possible significance of Russian power in the struggle with the Turks for free Eastern trade.

Certainly, Moscow was not yet ready for broad participation in European politics. Muscovy was still building its edifice of state, and had only just completed its main walls. It was still thoroughly engrossed in the interior finishing work even as it bulked the foundations of its new political order and organized its might and resources. Nevertheless, the end of the fifteenth century was a moment of the greatest significance for all of Europe. A new state was stepping forward onto the historical scene.

CHAPTER ONE

THE GREAT RUSSIAN PEOPLE

GREAT RUSSIA

The Muscovite state, from its very inception, was the political focus of Great Russia.[1] The nucleus which made the formation of this political organization easier was the Rostov-Suzdal region, limned geographically on the map of Eastern Europe by a broad belt of forests. It occupied approximately the area between the Volga and Oka rivers, the basin of the Kliazma and Northern Volga rivers from the mouth of the Tvertsa to the mouth of the Oka. The area was surrounded to the east by the Vetluga forest, to the north by the forests along the watershed between the Volga and Northern Dvina basins, to the west by the Oka forest and the forests and marshes between the Mologa and the Sheksina rivers, and on the south by the forested expanses that connect the Bryn and Murom forests. From the south the territories of Riazan and Chernigov Seversk adjoined it, from the west the lands of Smolensk and Novgorod. On the north was the territory of Novgorod the Great, and the eastern lands were inhabited by Finnish tribes.

An indigenous political life sprang forth there in the Rostov-Suzdal realm, "downstream" from Novgorod the Great and called "beyond the forest" by the Kievans from the moment Vladimir Monomakh[2] had sent his son Yury, called Dolgoruky[3] or the "Long Arm," to reign in the Rostov principality. Only from the time of that event in the 1120s do Russian chroniclers present any information whatsoever about the Russian lands of the Northeast. This state of knowledge about the most ancient ages in Great Russian life has fostered the illusion that the lands of Rostov in the twelfth century were more foreign than Russian, and that they were colonized anew during the era of Yury Dolgoruky and his son Andrei, thanks to the leadership and initiative of princely authority. Actually, it is not difficult to observe, through a more careful analysis of northern chronicles, features in North Russian life under Yury Dolgoruky and Andrei Bogoliubsky[4] which witness a considerable complexity in society in Rostov in the twelfth century.

Influential and prosperous boyars[5] stood beside the princes. The town centers, even those of secondary importance, were embellished with gleaming stone churches, whose architectural forms and sculptured decorations provide one of the most significant pages in the history of ancient Russian art. Both the value of the building materials, which had to be brought from the Kama river via the Volga, and the execution of the unique artistic style, indicate a level of local physical and cultural development which would be unimaginable had the conditions been those of a newly-colonized, barbaric land. The powerful local landowning boyars provoked Andrei Bogoliubsky to join a cruel struggle in which he perished. After his death the rule of the boyars materialized in the form of internecine wars seeking to usurp princely authority, features of the same social and economic order then experienced in southern Russia. Throughout Russia the eleventh century was a time of growing land ownership by the boyar class, accompanied by increasing boyar influence and privileges. In the Great Russian North the foundations of a social order were then emerging which would characterize it throughout the following centuries.

By the twelfth century events in the Russian Northeast posed a threat sufficient to demand the special attention of the prince.[6] The first princes to arrive found no place as leaders of peaceful colonization; rather, they encountered the unsettled conditions of an international travel route. Great Russia had spread out along the ancient commercial artery of the Volga river. Its early princes evolved a unique set of outside interests, which largely remained the same for several centuries, centering in the urge to control the East-West routes between the Baltic Sea and the Volga region. Crucial to this control was the hegemony of these downriver princes over Novgorod the Great, and the maintenance of free commercial and colonization routes to the southeast and east, down the Volga and towards non-Russian lands as far as the Urals, whose natural riches beckoned.

Over the course of two generations the political silhouette of Great Russia assumed a definite, although still elementary and weakly-sketched form. Russia now consisted of two mighty political systems—Novgorod and Rostov-Suzdal. During the age of Yury Dolgoruky the territory of Rostov underwent an experience typical of the early history of Great Russia. The center of power shifted from the city of Rostov to the city of Suzdal, just as under Andrei Bogoliubsky it again shifted, this time to Vladimir.[7] The princes entered into the conquest of the southern borderlands, including the Oka river basin and territories belong to Riazan and Chernigov. Under Vsevolod III[8] called the "Big Nest", the Great Russian principality gained further definition, its center at Vladimir on the Kliazma river-Vladimir-beyond-the-Forest. At this moment the meaning of the title "grand prince" found its true significance as a political title and the confines of his realm were drawn, becoming the limits of the Great Russia of that time. Vsevolod III succeeded in subjugating entirely the Riazan princes, and at one interval his appointed governors[9] ruled all the lands of Riazan. He enjoyed the same success with the princes of Murom. Novgorod itself fell under the sway of the grand prince, who sent his sons and nephews there to reign. The Russians of that era now grew aware of a unified political entity, which they called "the grand principality of Vladimir and Novgorod the Great."

Indeed, these two polities were connected by strong political and economic bonds. The commercial routes of Suzdal were essential arteries for Novgorod's trade; to Novgorod goods flowed from the Kama river region, from the Riazan lands, and from Suzdal itself. In turn, commodities came from the west and south; without grain from the trans-Volga regions Novgorod could not have survived. Unrestrained trade with Great Russia at large was the prerequisite of Novgorod's well-being and provided a powerful lever to the "downriver" princes in supporting Novgorod's independence from the center at Vladimir. For their part, the grand princes at Vladimir took on the responsibility of defending the western regions. The commercial centers of Novgorod and Pskov could not survive through their own strength alone. They depended upon the support of the grand prince and his military leaders[10] in the struggle against the advancing Swedes and the Germans of Livonia.[11] The same held true to the south. Battles against the nomads of the steppes and eastern Finnish tribes placed constant pressure on the forces of Riazan and Murom, and the support of the rest of Great Russia was just as essential for those principalities as it was for Novgorod. At this early stage in Great Russian history it was economic interest and the need for security from outside enemies that created the first and still immature forms of unity under a single political leadership.

The common schematic, and superficial, view in Russian historiography holds that the subsequent development of Great Russian life was one of fragmentation of territories and authority, of the formation of a clutch of petty principalities, and of the disintegration of what is termed the appanage-patrimonial system. At the same time other forces and tendencies were unifying socio-political life. Actually, these processes did not alternate; rather, they transpired as parallel, competing elements in a see-saw conflict. These processes were native to the development of the life and society of the Great Russian grand principality.

FOREIGN RELATIONS

For proper understanding of these features it is essential to keep in mind that they developed under the strong pressure of, and

in constant subjection to, foreign relations in Great Russian
national life. For example, the raids of Khan Batu[12] dealt a
convulsive blow to the grand principality of Vladimir. The main
victims of the massacre were the localities with large populations in the eastern part of the Vladimir realm. These areas still
had not recovered as late as the end of the thirteenth century
because of harassment by their Tatar neighbors, the terrible
suppression of popular unrest, and the burdens imposed by
Batu's tributes and taxes. At the end of the fourteenth century
the population wandered to the west, spawning the "young"
cities Tver and Moscow, towns which brought significant territories under their control. Vassalage to the Golden Horde
greatly hindered Great Russia's eastern march and halted for
many years military advances and colonization to the southeast.
Commerce beyond the Volga did not revive until after mid-
century, and then slowly and painfully. This revival brought
with it new claims to the eastern Finnish lands and aggressive
struggle with foreign neighbors. Great Russia's relations with
southern Russia also faded. To the west, independent Novgorod
the Great became stronger; its free people pursued their economic interests without restriction in their northern districts.
At least temporarily, they were exempt from taxation of their
commercial income by the Great Russian government.

That government had been weakened greatly. Its scope of
operations was sharply attenuated and the authority of Vladimir as a ruling center had fallen. Its last bright flash of energy
had been the activities of Alexander Nevsky,[13] who had battled
to defend the western regions from the Swedes and Livonian
Germans. Even this success was made possible by political restraint and cautious submissiveness to the Tatars. Under Alexander Nevsky the "Tatar yoke" was organized and the attend-
ant tribute rendered by the vassal Russian realm; the Tatar khan
held supreme authority over the Russian princes. Russo-Tatar
relations fell into a definite pattern. Recognition of the khan's
suzerainty over Russia earned the confirmation of the princes'

authority, and thereby allowed the princes to become inter-
mediaries between the Horde and Russia. The Russian princes
undertook to collect the taxes and pay the Tatars their tribute.
The positive effect of their intercession was to eliminate direct
Tatar involvement in governing the Russian lands. In these new
circumstances Russian political activities gradually expanded,
rekindling the thought of a geographic center which might
unify Russia's strengths and interests. Vladimir had not recovered from the general catastrophe it had suffered. Even
the leadership of Great Russia's international affairs, including
relations with the Golden Horde and border defense, slipped
away from the grand princes of Vladimir. Individual local officials began to establish their own arrangements directly with
the Horde. Conflicts with belligerent neighbors lay as a heavy
burden on the border areas of Great Russia, which began to
organize themselves as independent military forces and political entities.

In northeastern Russia the pressures of self-defense brought
increasing importance to the larger principalities of Tver, Riazan, and Nizhny Novgorod. The foreign relations of Great
Russia literally were divided among these strong principalities.
Local interest encouraged Tver to take responsibility for the
struggle against Lithuania, protection of Novgorod the Great,
and support of commercial and cultural ties with the West.
Riazan defended its territory from restless neighbors in the
steppes, preserving the southern borders of the forest zone in
the upper Don basin for Russian settlements. Only toward the
middle of the fourteenth century did the eastern part of Great
Russia recover from profound decay. The center of its renais-
sance was Nizhny Novgorod, which drew into its sphere the
remains of the former Suzdal principality. This larger entity
then vied with the restive border peoples and trans-Volga Tatars for trade and colonization routes. Yet in their isolation
all these border groups were unable to cope with the tasks

that fell to them. Compelling military demands forced them to seek allies in central Great Russia.

POLITICAL UNITY

The traditions of unity in a single large principality enjoyed a bright new vitality thanks to the popular recollections of Grand Prince Vsevolod III and Alexander Nevsky. At the very beginning of the fourteenth century Prince Michael Yaroslavich of Tver made a fitful attempt to revitalize that unity. He cultivated ties with the leading groups in society, the metropolitanate[14] of the Russian Orthodox Church, now in Vladimir, and the boyar class of Vladimir. Michael received the title of "grand prince of all Russia" and sought to take control of the chief cities in the realm, Novgorod the Great, Nizhny Novgorod, Vladimir, Pereiaslavl, and Kostroma. His attempt was foiled by the opposition of Moscow and Novgorod the Great. Riazan was too weak for such endeavors, but it pressed north toward the Oka river, whose shoreline was to serve for a long time as the chief Great Russian line of defense against dangers from the south. Riazan attempted to maintain fortified outposts beyond the Oka as well. Soon, however, it lost Kolomna and other districts to the merciless expansion of Moscow. Nizhny Novgorod's grand princes, like those of Tver, sought to deepen and expand their might by usurping the grand princedom. Complete failure awaited them. Tver and Riazan along with Nizhny Novgorod remained merely foreposts of Great Russia. The prince of Moscow, who from the time of Ivan Kalita[15] held the title of grand prince of all Russia, assumed the leadership of the burgeoning realm. Moscow princes tied anew the scattered threads of Great Russian foreign relations into a singular pattern.

Moscow's historical role was determined primarily by its politically strategic importance. Lasting warfare on three fronts fueled the drive to centralize authority in Great Russia and compelled the unification of Great Russia around Moscow.

The character of Russia's political organization found its basis in the subordination of the entire social fabric and all resources of the country to the powerful and unlimited central government of the grand prince. Naturally, this form of rule was the product of a long and persistent struggle, which found in strong and durable Moscow a new focus and rallying point. The Moscow princes had cause to consider this struggle to be a battle for preservation of the tradition of the grand principality, and for the satisfaction of the ancient claims of the senior prince to primacy among the fraternal princes of Russia, to patriarchal authority, and to "the seat of the father." The scribes and chroniclers[16] were right when they extolled Alexander Nevsky or Vsevolod III, and in a more distant time, Vladimir Monomakh, as the precursors of this urge toward a strong central authority under the grand prince.

It was not until the fourteenth century that conditions developed in the Great Russian ethnic region of Northern Russia that were essential to foster political unity. There the populace grew unified thanks to the hostility of neighboring tribes with organized military forces. No longer might this population migrate, for it had lost its freedom to resettle, a factor in the colonization of the Eastern European plain responsible for the extreme instability of the historical underlay of Ancient Russia. The people were constrained to seek their own territorial and political security and to wage protracted warfare for clearly defined borders. In the west they faced Swedish assaults on the Novgorod districts, the advances of the Livonian Germans toward Pskov, and most threatening, the thrusts of the Lithuanian Russian state from the west.[17] Meanwhile, on the southern and eastern flanks, combat continued with the Tatars and eastern Finnish tribes. These peoples maintained unrelenting pressure on the Russian forces and gradually compelled them to rally for self-defense and pursuit of greater freedom of trade, commerce and colonization. All of these factors were crucial for the safeguarding of the foundations of national economic life.

Following the initial flareup during the thirteenth century, the era of Ivan Kalita's son, Grand Prince Semen Ivanovich,[18] witnessed the onset of the conflict between Russia and Lithuania. While Dmitry Donskoy reigned the battles against the Tatar states grew in number, and the perennial defense of Novgorod and Pskov from "Germans," as the Swedish and Lithuanian forces were called, required the might of the grand princes of Great Russia. The alternative was to lose the trade cities that nourished the further economic and cultural interests of Great Russia. In addition, the methodical, progressive advances of Russian colonization into the Finnish Northeast offered trade benefits worthy of active organizational support.

This foreign affairs agenda confronting the central Great Russian state originated in its geographic and intertribal situation, and foreign affairs in turn determined that state's militant and authoritarian character. Under the pressure of these circumstances the entire process of the social and political organization of the Great Russian people took place.

CHAPTER TWO

PUBLIC LIFE IN THE GREAT RUSSIAN NORTH

COLONIZATION

The history of Russia is the story of a country undergoing colonization. Now reaching into empty lands and now retreating before fierce Asiatic hordes, in the flows and ebbs of the colonization movement the Eastern Slavs steadily occupied the territories of the broad Eastern European plain, then crossed its frontiers to settle the distant Eurasian expanses. The chief political accomplishments of the Eastern Slavs, such as the Kievan state or the consolidation of the Muscovite state, occurred when powerful foreign enemies forced the populace into more or less constricted territory, inspiring unity in self-defense. With success the Russian people turned aggressively against their hostile neighbors to seize the pathways of further colonization. Over the centuries the correlations between the total population and the territory it occupied did not favor intensive economic or social progress. The inadequacy of the nation's human and material resources to resolve practical domestic and foreign problems was a constant and indeed tragic feature of Russia's historical fate.

The result was that significant historical achievements were accomplished only at the cost of extreme exertion. The need for national organization necessarily took precedence over creative labors and the natural development of public affairs fell victim to the need to devote the entire strength and resources of the country to political necessities. In addition to the tension caused by Great Russia's international problems, the domestic situation of the country was shaped also by the poverty of the agricultural soil into which the socio-political edifice was being sunk. In a country rich in forests and water but with meager

growing soil, the farm populace was forced to wrest their piti-
ful fields from nature, and to settle in small villages on carefully chosen sites, far from neighbors.

Consequently, forest and water crafts held high significance,
including hunting, fishing and beekeeping. These endeavors
expanded the range of settlement as the people sought out
virgin clearings and meadows. The first methods of working
the soil were impermanent and fitful; the depleted fields were
readily deserted as the populace moved on to new lands in
search of more favorable conditions. Groups scattered in small
settlements spread over vast unoccupied tracts and, retaining
contact with their neighbors, formed large rural districts.[1] The
sparsely populated territory of these districts was enormous
in land surface but poorly delimited and weakly organized.
Boundaries were determined by the most distant settlements;
the unworked forests and lands long lay undemarcated between
adjacent districts as free land for the taking. Enterprise filtered
far and wide across the land, but did not penetrate deeply
into the expanse it embraced because of the predominance of
temporary tillage and dispersed settlement. Gradually yet inexorably colonization sapped the national strength by hinder-
ing consolidation. The benefits of consolidation arrived only
as the positive side effects of conflicts with those foreign enemies who halted further Russian settlement.

In the thirteenth and fourteenth centuries the people of
northern Russia found themselves in a political and geographic
situation that greatly retarded their movement by confining
them to a more or less limited territory. Colonization assumed
a different face as the people began to settle the back country
of districts already lightly occupied. New villages and outposts
sprang up throughout large districts, while new domains and
clearings appeared in previously unsullied forest depths. Frequently settlers were dispatched tens of versts away from their
homesteads, beyond marshland and forest. Having grown and
multiplied in strength and formed villages and outposts, they

would constitute a new small sub-district which then might become an independent district. In some circumstances settlements would cluster more densely whereupon the district would emerge as a more populous and durable presence.

THE PEASANT COMMUNE

The Great Russian peasant commune enjoyed a unique and rather complex existence. The interests which bound groups of settlements into large contiguous districts were partially economic, partially administrative and traditional. Economic functions, both agricultural and craft-related, were conducted on individual farmsteads and in small settlements which apportioned and shared their land use privileges. On the other hand, the problems of the use of forests, pastures, and new land tracts, as well as of new colonial undertakings, spawned a form of regulatory direction which was the business of the peasant commune. The elder[2] and the peasants of a commune represented the authority of the commune in matters concerning landholdings and the distribution of wilderness, forests, and lands that were not the property of individual households, or had been abandoned or deserted. A new settler was supposed to receive a parcel of land from the commune so that he would have a legal property claim. The commune also defended its lands against seizure by outsiders. Since the commune desired to augment its labor force and financial strength, it was interested in attracting new settlers to empty lands. The elected elder might lure new settlers with incentives such as tax exemptions, and leased pastures and forests for annual fees. These activities were connected to the service and dues obligations[3] imposed on the rural district communes. The ancient financial tribute rendered to the prince or ruler grew more defined and burdensome when it was combined with the required tribute to the Horde. Districts inhabited by poor bonded peasants were required to collect funds according to properties and trades, based on the ability of each to pay. The sum was gathered and handed to agents of the prince's government. Each commune member held joint responsibility for the other, those who had property for those who did not, the industrious inhabitants for those with empty fields.

At the same time, to an important degree the commune was a closed self-governing society. Its concerns were those of preserving domestic tranquility and order, of law enforcement and settlement of disputes and conflicts between neighbors. The princely administration was extremely ineffectual. The prince entrusted the court and the government to his town and rural lord lieutenants[4] who seldom were assigned a single district but most often several. The appointees of the lord lieutenant functioned with small staffs of six or less regional officials and constables[5], with responsibility for territory covering hundreds of versts. Only the most important matters concerning such crimes as murder, robbery, or thievery caught in the act, reached their attention. Other daily occurrences were handled in the communes. The communes also participated directly in the lord lieutenant's court. The peasants of the rural communes were responsible for preventing criminal acts by tracing, arresting and extraditing to the regional lord lieutenant "known wrongdoers, professional robbers and horse thieves." The peasants were held accountable for investigating every incident and might be fined for failure to locate a dangerous criminal. The fine might be levied on the entire commune and might amount to the sum imposed on the criminal himself.

PROVINCIAL ADMINISTRATION

The component parts of the district, the towns and villages, were bound to it by both taxation and the law. The district elders themselves provided all materials necessary for investigation and prosecution, and in addition they were well versed in their own common rights, their customs and traditions. The elected district officials thus were essential members of the regional courts, without whom the lord lieutenant could not convene his deliberative body. The commune was also active in satisfying the spiritual needs of the populace as well. The peasant commune provided the means for building churches, housing priests and other clerical aids, and provided their maintenance. Parish life was tightly intertwined with the district's daily pursuits, as was the life of small monasteries that at times were completely under the control of the district peasants who contributed to them.

With such varied activities all conducted by the district communities, the direct involvement of the prince's government and its institutions in rural affairs remained superficial and formal for many years. The princely authorities devoted their administrative efforts almost exclusively to exploiting the labor of the people to acquire the resources needed by the government. This they accomplished by organized collections and through enforcement of the work obligations owed by the populace. The regional administrators of the principality performed the vital assignment, in addition to their governmental functions at the local level, of pursuing the political goal of consolidating princely hegemony in the local districts. Such posts also rewarded the best servants of the prince. The local population was charged with the upkeep of the regional administrator, his agents, servants and family, by providing him with sufficient maintenance[6]. This obligation gradually took on the character of the prince's salary for service, the more so since the official usually received fees taken from government collections and taxes. Receipt of such payment necessarily transformed the regional administrator into a kind of tax collector or sharecropper on the princely holdings. A procedure evolved whereby a boyar who governed a district would forward half of the income to the treasury of the prince. When leaving the prince's service he would receive a prorated sum, or else agree to serve on until the time when accounts for contributions in kind to the prince were usually prepared, after the fall harvest period. Apparently, a period of one year was the customary unit for determining this salary of maintenance. Payments might be postponed from year to year, until the prince dismissed the boyar or the latter resigned from the administrative post. Later a priority system for maintenance payments evolved whereby at first a new appointee received advances prior to the stipulated period of service; later two or three persons together were given part of their income from duties, then maintenance went to son after father,, and nephew after uncle. These features of the economic relationship between princely rule and the administration of regional governors were typical of the entire structure of princely rule of state and people.

CHAPTER THREE

EMERGENCE OF THE GREAT RUSSIAN STATE

THE PRINCES OF RUSSIA

At the court of the prince and in the social circles surrounding it, from early Kievan times the concept evolved that the principe-dom was a family fief. Ancient Russia knew only reigning princes; each petty prince entertained pretensions to a "part of the Russian land,"[1] more precisely to a portion of his father's realm, which was the heritage of his father and grandfather before him. This interpretation of the right of princes stood in contrast to the poorly centralized society of Russia and strong sectional interests which led each city of any significance to seek a independent status under its local prince. At the other extreme, the princes occupying the high central ground of national political life sought, as "senior of all fraternal Russian princes," to retain control of the regional principalities by sending younger brothers, sons and nephews to reign there. The senior princes sought to maintain and enhance the existing political structure by citing the patriarchal authority of the father over the sons, the senior prince over other princes, and the principle *in loco paternis*. The development of regional society and the claims of the numerous younger princes to their ancestral lands destroyed unity when the significance of Kiev as the heart of ancient Russia's commercial and political life weakened and withered.

When it separated from the Kievan South, Great Russia structured its grand principality, now centered in Vladimir, along the familiar lines of local princely realms united under the authority of a grand prince. But it should be noted that during the twelfth and thirteenth centuries, the impotence of the senior or grand prince, as he was called in the North, grew evident to all of Russia. No longer was he capable of upholding the patriarchal, *in loco paternis* character of his rule. Consequently, the grand prince was recognized merely as an "elder brother" in the political terminology of the period; the less senior princes resolutely insisted upon their fraternal equality. The grand prince must consider them as younger brothers, not as subjects. He was not to hand orders to them but was to recognize their independent princely rights and authority. Matters of common interest must be resolved through consultation and by mutual consent. At that time influential elements in society opposed the strengthening of the power of the grand prince. Andrei Bogoliubsky's attempt to smash the independence of the junior princes and to subordinate the boyars ended in his demise, the outcome of a conspiracy of those very boyars. Andrei's brother Vsevolod III enlarged his authority in a struggle with princely relatives and the boyars, and finally established the grand principality of Vladimir. It is no wonder that he was called "the big nest," for his sons and grandsons followed the old Kievan traditions of mutual relations between princes. The Tatar invasion and the rule of the Golden Horde ruptured and smothered Great Russia at the very moment of birth. After the death of Alexander Nevsky the significance and might of the grand principality of Vladimir diminished, then crumbled under the pressure of the khan's rule into domestic scuffling for control of the grand princely mantle. But, by the 1330s, the struggle changed character to become one centering on the rise of Moscow.

CONSOLIDATION OF MUSCOVY

Moscow set about gradually strengthening the central Great Russian government and unifying Northern Russia through clash of arms on three fronts. These events determined the complexities of the political map of Great Russia. Only the small territories of Vladimir were subjected directly to the authority of the grand prince of Moscow. To these could be added only the traditional lands of Moscow's princes. Lesser principalities were closely allied to the grand principality for their princes had been subjected by Ivan Kalita and Semen the Proud. These included Rostov, Belozersk, Starodub, Galich and others. Their princes had lost almost completely their role in Russia's political life, but they "reigned and ruled" independently in their own small appanages. Reluctantly foregoing broader political aspirations, they were immersed in local administrative matters, chiefly with agriculture-related patrimonial jurisdictional affairs and mediation of disputes. Meanwhile, with each passing generation the princely territories fragmented until some were no larger than the hereditary estate holdings of a rich boyar. Along the frontiers of Great Russia the situation was different thanks to broader interests and outlooks caused in part by either belligerent or peaceful relations with neighboring peoples. Political configurations consequently were of greater size there, and less dependent on the central authority at Vladimir. For example, there were the grand principalities of Tver, Riazan, and Nizhny Novgorod with their own "grand princes" and lesser princes vying for local control. To the northwest, the popularly-ruled Novgorod the Great and Pskov enjoyed autonomy in their domestic affairs, although they accepted the hegemony of the "grand prince of all Russia."[2] Each of these entities exercised political influence and maintained military forces, and each beseeched the support of the Great Russian principality at the risk of their own forced subjugation to the grand prince at Vladimir. At other times they opposed him to protect local autonomy, even at the price of foreign alliances and vassaldom under the Lithuanians or strained ties with the Tatars.

In those tense international circumstances, coloring the affairs of Great Russia in the fourteenth and fifteenth centuries, the primary efforts and aspirations of the grand prince's government were directed toward uniting all military forces of

the country and all material resources under one central command for the purpose of organizing the defense of the travel
routes essential for developing the domestic economy. These
policies were intended to promote expansion and strengthen
the government. The unfailing aim of the agreements that the
grand princes made with other reigning princes was that of
gathering the country's domestic might and taking control of
all facets of its foreign relations. Yet in this historical enterprise the grand princes were restricted not only by the counter-
measures of the stronger local rulers, but also by the structure
of family and ancestral relationships in their own princely
court at Moscow. The principality of Moscow, the fulcrum of
all their activities, was a fief of the Danilovich family.[3] Upon
the death of the father, the head of family was the dowager
princess. Her sons were not to escape her will, including the
eldest who was now the grand prince of all Russia. The brother
princes ruled their ancestral lands according to a division of
territory decreed by their father in his last will. In principle
the brothers were to share equally, although this was violated
in Moscow in favor of the eldest. Since the time of Ivan Kalita
it had become customary for the eldest son to rule over the
most important military strongholds, such as Kolomna and
Mozhaisk. Furthermore, the brothers ceded to the eldest, the
grand prince, a portion of excess incomes from court revenues
and the Moscow city tax collections. The division of the patrimony did not fragment the realm into separate parts. Subse-
quently it signified the holding of appanages belonging to the
general inheritance, which did not break each prince's legal
connection to the whole. The appanages were hereditary, going
to the prince's sons and widows at his death; however, he did
not enjoy the right freely to dispose of his hereditary holdings
should he die without heirs. Such a portion of the general
patrimony would be returned to the family, to be divided
among the remaining brother princes. This redivision was conducted by the dowager princess, or by the eldest brother,

with the agreement of the younger princes, if their mother was deceased.

THE APPANAGE SYSTEM

According to the property laws it was possible to make a partial redivision under the supervision of the family to rectify losses suffered by one family member for whatever reason, in order to restore the proportional division of ancestral lands. The princes ruled, judged and preserved order on their appanages with complete independence, but in the general affairs of the entire principality they were to act in concert, according to specific traditions of "advice and counsel."[4]

The basic features of appanage rule over a common ancestral principality repeat the structure of peasant tenure of agricultural land. Their common failing was considerable instability, since only fraternal princes accepted it and agreement collapsed in the third generation. By that time the territory had disintegrated into individual and separate patrimonies that had lost the bonds imposed by the appanage system. Such disintegration developed unhindered wherever there was no strong outside counterforce to motivate united political action and struggle. The Moscow principality at times utilized this method of portional land tenure. The sons of Ivan Kalita ruled by the appanage system while maintaining a centralized army and financial administration. By the time of Kalita's grandsons and great grandsons there were two distinct patrimonies, Moscow-Kolomna and Serpukhov. The military unity of former years was replaced by treaty agreements for joint undertakings, while separate administrations emerged to deal with those in the population subject to taxes and to collect revenue from smaller principalities. The payments to the grand prince's treasury were continued solely because of the necessity for paying tribute to the khan.

The progressive disintegration of the ancestral lands in Moscow as elsewhere was halted by a situation wherein the eldest

prince of the Moscow family became at the same time the grand
prince of all Russia. Thereupon the domestic affairs of Moscow
grew closely dependent on the grand prince's policies and sway.
These policies also influenced the actual apportionment of appanage lands. Dmitry Donskoi[5] had determined that the most
important area, that of Kolomna, always should belong to
the grand prince's throne. A number of agreements provided
for family unity in foreign relations, military affairs and tribute
collection. But at the same time the family ancestral traditions
set strong limits to the power of the grand prince, and dependency on them contradicted the underlying trend in government toward autocracy. The conflict emerged with particular
sharpness as political life developed and in connection with the
prince's traditional claims to authority. In his last will and
testament Dmitry Donskoi laid the foundations for expanding
his hereditary rights to include all the territories of the grand
principality of Vladimir. The crucial question was whether the
grand principality and all the newly-acquired and conquered
lands would become the common patrimony of the family, to
be distributed in appanages. Contemporary opinion tended to
answer the question positively, and lesser princes more than
once voiced the demand that the grand prince divide new lands
among them. Dmitry Donskoi acceded to these traditional conceptions by granting his younger sons, in addition to portions
of the Moscow lands, additional territories of the grand prince.
Serious disputes arose thereafter between his sons concerning
land jurisdiction, and grew into a grave crisis in relations among
the princes. A struggle followed over succession to the grand
princely authority. The disputes extended to other mutual relations between the grand prince and his relatives, and more
distant fraternal princes.

THE GRAND PRINCE OF MOSCOW

The grand prince and his rule could become a major political
force only by breaking away from the system of traditional

patrimonial rights. The grand prince accomplished this goal by simply violating the tradition in practice; when this proved successful, he was able to reject the former procedure in principle. The grand prince held a significant advantage over the younger princes in that, besides his share of the Moscow inheritance, he also controlled the forces of numerous petty princes whom he had been able to transform into princes owing him military service.[6] In the final analysis his superiority could not fail to rend the governing structure of the Moscow princely family.

The grand princes insistently pressed for the subjugation of appanage holdings to their supreme will. The individual ancestral rights of lesser princes were to give way to an allotment system guided by the grand prince's will and favor. The disposition of all territory was concentrated in his hands, and control of intestate lands reverted to him without redistribution. He was the lord of all members of the family, including the dowager princess. This new version of the grand prince's authority gradually evolved through a series of blows to the old established structure. The successors of Dmitry Donskoi moved resolutely to destroy former family relationships. They seized vacant appanage lands and did not divide them with their brothers. They changed the composition of their territorial holdings by forced exchanges of rural districts, distributing them at will as appanages and hereditary lands. Then the grand princes demanded that the lesser princes abandon their independent political roles and accept total subjugation in foreign affairs, military matters, and apportionment of tribute collection. The same procedure was applied to the ancestral holdings of petty ruling princes on the territory of the grand principality of Vladimir. The grand princes obtained from them the repudiation of hereditary rights in their own favor. The appanage rulers kept their lifetime tenure but relinquished posthumous succession rights in exchange for rewards of one kind or another (as in the notorious "purchases" of Ivan Kalita).[7] Later a different form appeared: a ruling petty prince would turn his patrimony over to the grand prince who in return would grant him back the same land for life, at times with additional territory, at times with less. Prior to the death of such an hereditary prince, semi-voluntary reverter arrangements of this kind sometimes were reinforced by statements inserted in the prince's will that his patrimony was to accrue to the grand prince. This was followed by a request for prayers for his soul and a request that his debts be forgiven.

Such wills presented the opportunity for Russian historians to speak of the right of princes to make a last will and testament which disposed of their patrimonial or appanage holdings and the dying man's right to relinquish his personal property rights. In fact, these wills represent merely specific forms for disposing of ancestral property rights under pressure from the government of the grand prince. Such wills were not only written at the dictation of Moscow, at times they were edited directly by the scribes of the grand prince. This break with the past did not transpire without grievous disorders. It not only undermined the foundations of relations among the lesser princes but also severely shook the basic traditions and ethical bonds of fraternal "unity" among princes, and of their family relations, as the moral foundation of the age-old traditions so beloved during the Russian middle ages. The cruel disorders during the times of Vasily the Dark[8] [1425-1462] with their dramatic details of blinding captured rivals and poisoning indomitable foes, betrayal and private violations of oaths on the cross, bloody reprisals on an opponent's servitors[9] and greedy lust for the patrimonies of enemies—all these marked a period of painful change from the tired but still persistent traditions. The stark methods of liquidation used by the grand prince's government during that upheaval first introduced the spectre of the "terrible" tsar into life in Great Russia; the true embodiment of this terror came in the activities of Ivan III,

[1462-1505], his son Vasily III[10] [1505-1533], and the tsar who culminated all these dramas, Ivan the Terrible[11] [1530-1584].

On the ruins of the traditional structure of relationships as sanctified by the moral and legal customs of centuries grew the unified rule of the sovereign grand prince. The methods of the past gave way to the solitary will of the prince. The basis of such rule was found in the patriarchal, hereditary principle of rule over all the grand princely lands, embodying uniquely and completely the ancient tradition of the senior Russian prince as successor to the father. In the extreme it became the concept of the grand prince as sovereign over all sovereigns of the Russian land. He was autocratic in his absolutism, and free of all customary precedents save his own will as ruler.

IVAN THE TERRIBLE

Ivan III completed the destruction of the old patrimonial order by abolishing the former independence of the largest regional political units and converting all of Great Russia into his hereditary state. There remained a certain unfinished quality to the factually completed unification of power into a single state, for Pskov and Riazan retained apparent autonomy in political affairs. Although their vitality was long since spent, their autonomy was destroyed formally only by Vasily III. Even so, Ivan III gave full hereditary autocracy its sharpest expression in his attitude toward succession to the grand princedom. Following the example of his father, who had made him co-ruler as a youth, and the models of Byzantine practice, Grand Prince Ivan proclaimed his first-born son Ivan to be grand prince along with him.

The untimely death of Ivan Ivanovich[12] and his father's second marriage posed a complex problem for the court of the Muscovite grand prince. The young grand prince had left a son, Dmitry, who in the spirit of the Byzantine concept was the "royal born." The grandfather, with the agreement of boyars close to the court, recognized Dmitry's rights, sealing that recognition with a solemn church ceremony of annointment and ascension to the throne of the grand prince. But the plotting of Ivan III's second wife, the Byzantine princess Sofia,[18] and the struggle of court parties, changed Ivan's intentions in favor of his son from the second marriage, Vasily. Ivan, however, began with half measures. He proclaimed Vasily sovereign grand prince and gave him Novgorod and Pskov as his "grand principality."

Upset by the prospect of division and disorders, the people of Pskov directed a petition to Grand Princes Ivan and Dmitry imploring them not to divide their realm, and that the sovereign in Pskov be the same as the grand prince in Moscow. The Pskovians received a severe and characteristic reply. Angrily Ivan III declared his freedom to do with his grandsons and children, as well as with his lands, whatever he wished. He would grant a princedom to whomever he deemed worthy. Within two years he made good his threat by banishing his grandson Dmitry and placing his son Vasily on the throne, properly annointed by the church as autocrat of the grand principality of Vladimir and Moscow. Although united under Ivan III's autocratic rule, the recently independent territories were not yet merged into a unified state. Ivan III's terminology in his testament, for example, is ambiguous in naming the portions of his realm. The concept of the grand principality at times narrows to the boundaries of the Moscow-Vladimir lands (the state of Muscovy in the strict sense according to the common understanding of the sixteenth century). Elsewhere it expands to include the Novgorod region. A broader definition was given to the term "the entire grand princedom." Only the assumption of the title of tsar[14] provided a solution to these vacillations through the formulation "all lands of the Moscow tsardom." Here at last all hereditary power was drawn together at the center. Its autocratic bearer embodied that unity and could say, in complete harmony with the political conscience of his time: "L'état, c'est moi." "I am the state."

CHAPTER FOUR

THE PATRIMONIAL AUTOCRACY

ECONOMIC FOUNDATIONS

The quest for a unified state led to the concentration of the country's entire might in the hands of a single ruling authority. This became an inevitable necessity as foreign threats waxed and new complexity entered Great Russia's international security situation. Russia redoubled its efforts to escape the restricting borders that limited its economic life and colonization. The recentralization of government that followed the dilution of power during the era of appanage rule did not by itself provide sufficient might to the grand princedom. It was merely the essential prerequisite for greater and more complex organization. The entire order of princely governance lay too superficially on the life of the people, without penetrating into its depths or mastering its strengths. It was unable to find ways to regiment and exploit the people in pursuit of "affairs of state." The financial needs of the prince's government and administration were satisfied primarily by the court's own economic and agricultural activities: contributions in kind supported the military and administrative structures as did the development of extensive agriculture by the boyars. The tax collections were swallowed up by the tributes and other payments to the Tatars. Other receipts by the prince such as commercial taxes were simply insignificant.

The overall situation meant that the appanage financing procedures imparted an agricultural nature to the prince's government. The court household and the prince's farming activities attained major proportions and grew closely intertwined with the basic tasks and functions of administering the country. As everywhere in the thirteenth-fifteenth centuries, conventionally

known as the "Middle Ages," Russia's hereditary prince was not
only the governor but also the master in an economic sense.
The contours of his rule, so fundamentally and essentially differing from Russian social and juridical conceptions and including agricultural and political rights as well as economic and legal jurisdictions, blended into an arbitrary sphere of princely
competencies and might. Historians often call this unique structure (quite arbitrarily and incorrectly) the "confusion" of private and state rights; it might be more precisely labelled the
primary syncretism of the social and political functions of rule.
It was the source of the unhindered awards of administrative
power and of the hereditary nature the rule of the prince sub-
sequently assumed.

THE ROYAL ADMINISTRATION

In large principalities the prince's household acquired a complex structure. For administration it was divided into several
branches for specific activities. At the head of the court servitors and all the other persons living and working at the court
was the "major-domo," whose responsibility it was to administer the prince's agricultural undertakings, including his cultivated lands and his peasants living in court villages. He supervised the obligatory service of all types owed to the prince
through his agents, stewards, managers and village elders. The
master of the hunt administered the hunting and trapping preserves, dog kennels, and beaver ponds. There were separate court
offices for falconers, for horses including the stables and meadows, for beekeeping and other special estates and operations,
for court fishing preserves, gardens and vineyards, as well as
villages of fishermen, gardeners, vinekeepers, and all the peasants involved in such husbandry. Each court office had its own
lands scattered throughout the principality, and its own subject
population; each constituted not only an economic but a legal
and administrative unit, and its administrators directed that
population in all its affairs.

At the same time, the significance of the court offices extended beyond royal lands since they involved more than court peasants and workers. The administrative court offices also had duties that tied people outside the court system to the court household. These duties fell into the category of general labor assistance to the court office by the surrounding populace, including cutting hay on state meadows, flushing game for the hunt and driving fish, pasturing the prince's horses, feeding the princely hunting party when it passed on a royal hunt, and other obligations. As time passed these responsibilities increasingly were replaced by levies of money and produce (hay, other fodders, and the like).

Parallel to this administrative system growing out of the royal household's economic activities, an administrative network of governors and rural district officials formed. They received their maintenance from the local population and supervised the law courts, settled disputes, managed tax collections and the service duties of towns, nearby settlements, and obligated state or court peasant communes[1] . Apart and separate from the two systems of court and appointed administrators there was a third category composed of large hereditary agricultural holdings. Their owners were the chief mainstays of the grand prince-the boyars, and the clergy.

THE BOYARS

It is as impossible to imagine the Russian prince of the thirteenth-fifteenth centuries without his boyars surrounding him as it is to picture the Kievan prince of ancient Russia without his princely retinue[2] . The prince's chief source of power was to be found in his ties with the boyars. The first step of the government of the grand prince to consolidate power was to gather the most powerful boyars. The boyars of the grand principality of Vladimir, clustered around the grand prince's court and the seat of the metropolitanate, formed the social class that experienced more sharply than any other the dissipation of the strength of a united Great Russia in interminable domestic conflicts, military failures, and exhaustion in fighting off foreign enemies. The pressing interests of the boyars led this class to promote unifying tendencies and to support the idea of a single and stronger grand prince. This group believed that the drive for social authority and material privilege would be advanced by a close alliance with the ruler. Their established interests included concern for the well-being of the Russian land as they understood it. At the beginning of the fourteenth century the attempt by Michael of Tver[3] to create a "grand principality of all Russia" was stimulated by the boyars of the grand prince's entourage, who wished him to be their leader. Michael's failure and the exodus of the boyars to Moscow together with the metropolitan's suite contributed to the decisive success of the prince of Moscow. In him the boyars found the desired stable center around which the Great Russian military and governmental resources might be consolidated. Moscow waxed stronger also as it struggled with its rivals, sapping them of vital strength by attracting numerous boyars to its side. Urging them to depart other principalities for the service of Moscow, it secured these services by granting profitable subsistences and large patrimonial manors.

In granting cities and rural districts to boyars for their maintenance, the grand prince did not squander his power and incomes. Such grants were the sole available means for consolidating political mastery over a broad territory. It was impossible to bring the entire human and geographic expanse under court administration, which at that time represented the only system of direct royal control that could provide labor and income from the prince's dominions. Rather, the grand prince transferred minimum administrative authority for local affairs to appointed officials to oversee the service and fealty of the boyars, to collect a portion of the revenues of a region, and to implement his political control of the given territory and population.

In any politically organized society where even the most elementary administrative system has been developed there are relationships—the so-called threads of rule—which must be grasped if effective mastery of the country's vital forces is to be exercised. For Russia in the Middle Ages the boyar class comprised this essential web of relationships. The historical origin of the boyar class is a matter for debate. The boyars stood as a necessary element in the prince's government for organizing armies, conducting battles, and execution of administrative and legal affairs. No boyar class existed in ancient Russia beyond that serving the prince, and it was a nobility based on service. As the historical successor of the older retinue, (or "advising boyars" in the expression of the *Tale of Igor's Campaign*[4]), the boyars comprised the upper level of the royal court and included all personal servitors engaged in conducting the prince's political activities. The steady political ascent of Moscow produced a proportionally greater number of boyars concentrated at the court of the grand prince, bringing increasing complexity and pronounced stratification. As was the case with the ancient retinue, the influential members of the court of the grand prince were his voluntary or free servitors. They had entered the grand prince's service by petition[5] and had been accepted with the promise to heed their interests and maintain them during their periods of service. A voluntary and personal bond took shape which was considered to be a form of contractual agreement, although we have no knowledge of specific formal arrangements. Voluntary service was based on mutual interest, the moral concept of "fealty," the duty to "wish well in all things," and not "to contemplate harm." Concretely it was manifested in military service, participation in campaigns and defense, and politically in terms of counsel and government affairs. Voluntary service might be broken by "renunciation" and "departure" to the service of another prince.

Beginning with the fourteenth century it is possible to document the appearance of increasingly more precise terminology for defining various types of voluntary servitors. The term courtier indicated the members of the prince's court who were from the lower classes; they were considered as servitors under the majordomo. With the passage of time, however, more and more members of the lesser gentry came under this classification, so that the term itself acquired the new meaning of a middle level of free servitors. They were found not only at court, but in cities throughout the realm as well. There and in the rural districts they represented the remnants of the former hereditary gentry now ranked as small and intermediate service nobles. The word boyar acquired a more specific meaning connoting the upper stratum of free servitors, in contrast to Western Russia where, above that level, there were nobles referred to by the Polish term "pan." In West Russian areas the boyar level was equivalent to the Great Russian lesser gentry.[6]

PALACE BOYARS

The most important boyars in Great Russia at this time were known as "palace boyars." Such authoritative historians as Sergei M. Soloviev and Vasily O. Kliuchevsky have attempted to explain this term by defining it in terms of the duties expected of these boyars, but without clear success.[7] To be sure, palace boyars were found with prestigious responsibilities in the central and provincial governments, as chiefs of court departments, princely lieutenants, and city governors. Appointment to such offices did not, however, make the holder a palace boyar. It would be more proper to say that the grand prince, in surrounding himself with palace boyars, assigned them to these or other duties, including jurisprudence, military or civil administration, and management of court affairs, the treasury, or departments of his household.

The very concept of palace boyar and the contrived term itself evolved in a peculiar manner which enhanced the status of the boyars. As a common term it began to be applied to the servitors occupying the senior level at the princely court. This position distinguished the boyar from the ranks of other boyars, and especially from the free servitors in general. Historical sources do not explain the root of the term but give only the adjectival form [translated here as palace]; but it would be easy to picture the rank being bestowed at a solemn ceremony administered by senior boyars to a younger one being admitted to membership in the prince's council of advisers. This special group of palace boyars must have represented a stage in the emergence of the even more elite group of boyar councillors as the closest advisors and collaborators of the grand prince and his government.

The palace boyars comprised a circle of advisors to the prince, who entrusted them with vital functions in the courts and government. But the term did not last and gave way to the concept of boyar councillor. Once again those closest to the prince were honored as the highest stratum of nobility. The remaining boyars performed secondary responsibilities in the royal departments[8] and elsewhere. If they did not rise to the level of councillors they sank back into the ranks of free servitors, or fell to the level of the lesser boyars[9] and courtiers of the grand prince. The boyars did not constitute solely a service class. The foundation of their service position lay in their unique social authority; at the same time their influential service rank nourished, deepened and developed their social advantages and their influence as the principal landowners. Boyar land tenure in one measure or another sprang up early in the Kievan period;[10] beginning in the eleventh century there are reports of boyar villages where work was performed by slaves or indentured laborers.

CHURCH LANDHOLDING

To turn to church landowning, it should be noted that from
early times, following establishment of monastic properties
and the church hierarchy in Russia, church landownership had
been growing. In Russia this did not take the usual form of
church property as a whole and indivisible institution, but
rather followed the patterns of hereditary land tenure. In other
words, the properties belonged specifically to a certain monastery, metropolitanate, diocese, or even a cathedral or parish.
This fact imparted to church properties the character of hereditary boyar landholdings. The church held ownership rights
equal to the boyars in terms of both scope and structure.

THE PRINCELY ESTATES

Alongside the boyars and the church the greatest landowners
were the princes themselves, who from ancient times had developed their own personal agricultural and artisan economy.
The might of patrimonial land ownership lay in controlling the
means of production, including the labor force of slaves, livestock, grain reserves for "seed and consumption," and the
capability of outfitting new settlements. The organizational
leadership for colonizing vacant lands, exploitation of virgin
lands and establishment of operations in the wilderness were
all within the broad scope of wealthy landowners' activities.
The initial source of their wealth had not been economic. It
originated in seizure of captives in wartime, division of tribute
between the prince and his retinue, and thereafter trade with
the goods so obtained. Consequently the princes and the princely boyars assumed the leading role in commerce in ancient
Kievan Russia.

The prince's position of authority also served to further his
landholdings. To his lands came, for one reason or another,
persons who had abandoned their customary way of life,
including slaves who had bought their freedom, free men,

members of every variety of displaced social class, and free peasant laborers who had not been able to endure the difficult conditions of independent farming in their home rural districts. All of these people came to the lands of the prince seeking not only an assured livelihood but the protection of a powerful lord as well. Similar motives also attracted displaced persons to the lands of the church and monasteries, to which populated areas had passed from the prince's estates as land grants. At the dawn of the Kievan period, throughout Russia a powerful surge of boyar privilege and property ownership corresponding in type to the land ownership of the princes and the church was evident. Hereditary land rights, both secular and clerical, became a closed circle whose economic hallmark was the combination of extensive property with limited exploitation. In social and political terms, the patrimonial supervision and the legal and administrative power of the landowner expanded greatly over the entire population on his lands.

The economic, administrative, and political importance of patrimonial land ownership grew and became firmly entrenched in Northern Russia during succeeding centuries. The role of monastery and boyar land ownership was very significant for the advance of the domestic colonization of Great Russia. This was the wedge that penetrated rural territories, here turning the sod of unoccupied lands in the trackless wilderness, and there laying hold of lands and commons[11] that peasant communes "from ancient times" had considered their own. Frequently at first such seizures evoked no protests from rural community leaders. But as the hereditary landlords expanded and multiplied their control of hamlets and new villages, they increasingly blocked the development of peasant economic units and peasant utilization of common and virgin lands. In addition to land seizure, the advance of patrimonial possessions into the rural districts assumed other guises, such as buying developed lands from individual members of peasant communities. The rich neighbor who had purchased lands would then encourage part of the district populace to move to his estates in return for aid, loans and protective patronage. Having lost land, common holdings, and its vital human resources, the peasant rural community, weakened both socially and economically, would seek the protection of royal officials, complaining that its villages and rural territories were being taken by the boyars, metropolitans and monasteries. In deserting their own plots the inhabitants reduced the labor force and the community's taxpaying ability.

PATRIMONIAL LANDHOLDING

The patrimonial landowners, however, were too important to the prince to allow him to come to the aid of the rural communities in this conflict. N.P. Pavlov-Silvansky stated that "The boyar class truly was not only a landowning institution but also an administrative one."[12] The development of patrimonial landownership, accompanied by patrimonial political power, became an essential stage in the formation of the military might and the economic resources of the principality. It paralleled the system of royal departments and administration by appointed governors. The boyars and the clergy were two vital and influential pillars of the grand prince's government and as their role in society waxed they could count on the latter's concern for their interests. By supporting them the prince meanwhile strengthened his ties and influence with the leading levels of society. Both of these factors are involved in determining the nature of the policy of land grants.[13]

Clerical and secular patrimonial landowners found the legal justification for their seizures from rural communities in land grants received from the grand princes. The grand prince (as well as lesser princes) would authorize a clerical institution or his boyar to take over unused land and forests in a particular rural area, with the use of local common lands, deserted territories in the district, virgin land worked by settlers on lands

of peasant communities, and the like. The grants expressly forbade interference by communal elders or peasants. Not un-
commonly, such grants were distributed to confirm an existing situation accomplished through seizure or other acquisition
of land. In the event of disputes, popular common law in-
variably gave way to the hereditary rights granted by the prince.
In granting such rights the princely charters also permitted the
colonization of wilderness. Settlers, primarily from other principalities, could be invited with the stipulation that the number
of rural community laborers would not thereby be reduced.
Actual practice ignored such limitations, and from afar settlers
continued to flow to the hereditary lands. The prince's government tried in vain to counter the plunder of tax-obligated
lands and population. In the agreements of the fourteenth
century the princes agreed not to purchase lands that were
subject to taxes, nor to lure peasants off such lands into their
own service. Furthermore, gentry holding ancestral lands were
enjoined from such acquisitions. As it turned out, life itself
enfeebled these attempts.

No matter how diligently the appanage princes guarded their
own rights and incomes, the government of the grand prince
pursued its grant system. To obtain the services of the boyars
it granted them lands belonging to the court both for maintenance and as hereditary possessions. Populated areas with indentured communal peasants were included. This latter practice developed to its full extent only later, in the sixteenth and
early seventeenth centuries, when the system of military fiefs[14]
or service estates developed. Nevertheless, occasional grants of
inhabited lands to monasteries and service princes occurred
much earlier. The first example dates from 1130 when Prince
Mstislav Vladimirovich and his son Vsevolod presented a deed
granting the rural district of Buitsa to the Yuriev monastery of
Novgorod. These grants meant transfer of princely rights and
incomes in the given district, although the actual governance

of the land did not change. Such a distinction actually had little
practical significance.

In colonizing occupied lands, the major patrimonial landlords settled free men on them who had petitioned to be taken
as serfs[15]. On the colonized lands these formerly free men
merged with the serfs and indentured laborers of the patrimonial estate. They were linked not only by a common agricultural
organization, but also by their mutual subordination to the patrimonial authority. The grant charters of the grand prince established the right of the landlord to institute courts and settle
disputes, and released the residents on the estate from the jurisdiction of the crown governors and courts. Despite widely
held opinion to the contrary, these deeds did not in fact create
new rights and privileges. As. K.A. Nevolin states, they merely
confirmed the *status quo* that had come into being by evolution
and through common law dating from the most ancient times.
The written formulation of these ancient rights, however, and
their definition in the grant charters, lent them new importance
as circumstances changed. The recognition that vested rights
must be granted by the prince made such rights derive from the
crown as the acknowledged source of legitimate claims. The
medieval concept of grants, on the other hand, tied the grants
to an obligation of fealty to the prince and might be accompanied by specific compensatory demands. The utilization by
the grand prince's government of grant charters fostered the
view that the rights of grant holders were subject to the government's supreme will. The grants were to be renewed with every
change of ruler, and with every new landholder. As a consequence there occurred a gradual reevaluation of the terms of
the grants, accompanied by a general tendency toward limiting
the rights and privileges provided for in previous charters. Therefore the grant charters, while lending the major landlords support in their relations with other segments of the population,
at the same time preserved the landlords' subordination to the
grand prince. Consequently, the rights of the boyars eroded as

their independence was exchanged for delegated powers based on the grantor's favor.

This entire evolution of relationships had the purpose of resolving the fundamental contradiction between the hereditary powers of the prince throughout his realm and the similar patrimonial powers of the major landlords. The overall structure of these rights was so similar that the connection between boyar lands and the crown apparently rested on nothing other than the boyar's personal voluntary service to the prince. As a result, the right to repudiate such service and depart threatened to destroy the territorial integrity of the principality. Available sources contain little evidence to show that withdrawal of hereditary lands occurred during the Middle Ages in Russia, whether the landlord was a service prince or a free member of the retinue. This is primarily because the sources relate mainly to the principality of Muscovy and the period of rapid expansion of the grand prince's might. Withdrawal of hereditary lands from the principality was suppressed early in history, and the grand princes needed merely to eliminate the last vestiges of these practices in the political backwaters of Great Russia as these regions gradually came under their direct control. The documents available for studying these relationships reveal that the organic bond between voluntary service and independent hereditary land tenure had been broken already. A boyar who had withdrawn might serve a different prince while retaining his hereditary lands in the realm where formerly he had served. On the other hand, his lands were bound legally and for taxation purposes to the political jurisdiction of his former prince, and the boyar himself was obliged to come to that ruler's defense with his retainers in case of an enemy attack. The service obligations of the boyars were taking root and strengthening the links between service and the territorial suzerainty of the prince.

SERVICE AND LAND

In the fourteenth and fifteenth centuries agreements were reached between princes which tied boyar service to the principalities. In them, as far as possible, the grand princes pursued the goal of tying all active military forces and military leadership to the land grants rather than to the personal service obligation. They subjected the military service of the boyars of secondary principalities to their control wherever these lands comprised part of the territory of the grand principality. Furthermore, the grand princes acquired the right to punish those who withdrew from their realm.

The connection between service and land tenure was the foundation for the entire military structure of the Middle Ages. Service princes and boyars brought armed detachments raised from the population of their lands into the army of the grand prince. The personal departure of a boyar from the service of the prince could not and should not have been accompanied by a lessening of the military force he was obliged to provide. Because of the bond between service and land, it was natural that there developed a gradual suppression of the right to withdraw freely from service. This development necessarily followed the denial of the right to retain hereditary privileges when leaving the prince's service. It is true that treaties between princes long continued to guarantee the right of personal withdrawal from a prince's service, but such formulas doubtless survived without any real meaning as relics in the treaty texts, along with many other meaningless passages. Remnants of the right to leave service were considered tolerable between amicable and related princes, and between the grand princes and his lesser relations, but the broad number of free serving nobles lost the right early. They renounced the privilege of leaving service according to agreements, thereby applying this principle to the entire personnel of the princely court. Important service princes also relinquished this right by treaty.

The arbitrary departure of an individual from the service of the prince became tantamount to flight across the borders of the realm, and entailed the loss of all rights and bonds to the grand princedom. The paucity of historical sources permits no clear comprehensive picture of the gradual erosion of the right to withdraw from service, one of the perquisites of voluntary service. Certainly the process was completed by the time of Ivan III. Provisions in agreements denying withdrawal from service, which historians regard as to crucial to the question, are exceedingly rare. Ivan III obtained such a commitment from Prince Daniel Dmitrievich Kholmsky in 1474 when Daniel's brother Michael was still reigning in Tver; during the reign of Vasily III a similar obligation was required of the captured Lithuanian army commander, Konstantin Ostrozhsky, as well as from the princes Vasily Shuisky[16], the Belsky princes, Ivan Vorotynsky, Michael Glinsky, Ivan and Andrei Shuisky and Fedor Mstislavsky, all of whom previously had served the government of the grand prince. These commitments removed the last glimmers of the notion of free withdrawal from princely service, and obliged the service nobility to inescapable and life-long faithful service as members of the Moscow boyar class and of the court of the grand prince. The titled and untitled Moscow boyars accepted the service princes into their number upon declaration of the latters' future fealty to their own lord. The significance of these commitments is understandable only when the link of the boyars to the grand prince is fully appreciated, for it stood at odds with the attempts of newly-arrived magnates to consider themselves, as of old, free servitors of the prince.

MONARCHY AND PATRIMONY

In the second half of the fifteenth century hereditary landholding and voluntary service declined as the emergence of the hereditary monarchy of the grand prince took place. The boyars and lesser boyars joined the court nobility of the grand prince as equally "enslaved" servitors. This change in basic principles was perceived by society not as the replacement of voluntary personal service by obligatory subjection to the crown, but as a transition to personal dependence, complete and unconditional. The transition was completed in the sixteenth century. Baron Sigismund Herberstein,[17] who came as the ambassador of Emperor Maximilian to Moscow in 1517 and 1525, was struck by the autocracy of Grand Prince Vasily III. In his "Notes on Affairs in Moscow" Herberstein set down his impressions: "The power which he has over his subjects easily surpasses that of any monarch in the world. He has completed that which his father began, in taking away from all the princes and other landlords their cities and fortified places. He oppresses all equally with cruel bondage, so that if he orders anyone to attend at court or to go to war, or to serve as ambassador for some assignment, that person is compelled to fulfill the assignment at his own expense. He imposes his rule on clergy as well as laity, and deals unimpeded and wilfully with the lives and property of all."

Hereditary autocracy appeared to the foreign observer in the first quarter of the sixteenth century to be an accomplished fact. The mustering of princely power, bound by common-law relationships, not only united the Muscovite autocracy but also liberated it from the confines of ancient tradition and obligation, opening the way for utter autocratic rule. The sovereign grand prince enjoyed the full command of the human and material resources of the entire population, and in fact controlled the lives and property of all. This totality of power was the foundation of the enormous organizational endeavor that was to be accomplished by the government of the Muscovite state in the sixteenth century.

CHAPTER FIVE

THE BOYARS OF GREAT RUSSIA

CROWN GRANTS

During the epoch of voluntary noble service the bond between
prince and boyars was personal and based on petitions offering
service and expecting patronage. This was much as it had been
in the retinues of ancient Russia. The prince's men of old Russia
were separated from the general population as a distinct social
group under the power and protection of their prince. He was
their defender, punishing crimes against their lives and personal
immunity by extreme measures, while they fell under his jurisdiction in a special relationship outside the normal legal system. He was the source of their material well-being and security. In subsequent evolution, these venerable relationships determined the unique position of the boyars vis-á-vis the prince.
But personal service led to personal subordination. With the
blossoming of voluntary service, the personal bond to the prince
came to be regarded as a privilege. The major landowners, both
of the service nobility and the clergy, were exempted from the
jurisdiction of the prince's administrative institutions. Together
with the entire population of their patrimonial lands, they were
subject solely to the prince, and only the central law court sat
in judgement of their affairs. Grant charters endowed hereditary land ownership with the character of a grant from the
prince, and determined the extent and nature of the owner's
rights and privileges. The grants were of temporary duration,
exempting the hereditary property from payment of tribute
and other taxes, and thereby bolstered the colonizing potential
of major landholders. There are, however, among Great Russian
charters some few so-called "tarkhan" grants[1] providing total

financial privileges. Apparently such charters were of compara-
tively rare occurrence and were issued only to particularly influential and outstanding religious institutions.

A grant commonly was limited in both duration and scope
of privileges, which could be incomplete in two respects. It
might encompass less than the entire labor force of the hereditary lands, and include only new settlers, or else permit the
newcomers at least somewhat broader privileges than the long-
term residents. The financial privilege did not exempt the hereditary lands from payment of their share of the tribute to the
Golden Horde and the Tatars. Furthermore, the grants usually
specified a period of five to ten years with the stipulation that
upon expiration those who had benefited from the exemptions
were to be subject to the same obligations as long-time inhabitants of the lands, to the best of their ability as determined by
an assessment. To establish tax liabilities, a survey of properties,
livestock, and crafts production was taken among the peasants
of a given hereditary estate, resulting in calculation of the
general amount to be collected from them. Hence the grant
charters established not only rights and privileges, but eventually obligations as well.

THE COURT AT MOSCOW

Gradual unification of power in Great Russia in the hands of
the grand prince of Muscovy attracted the flower of the Great
Russian boyars to the core city of Moscow, which became the
focal point for service, administration, and social amenities for
the boyars. The personal service nobility of the grand prince
formed a part of his court. When not occupied with duties as
military and civil leaders, they lived in Moscow at the beck of
the grand prince. This estate-holding aristocracy was in all respects tied to service and its entire interests were chained to
the activities of the crown. The role in government of the
boyars contributed to the suppression of their liberties and

promoted ever closer links to the court of the grand prince. As of old, the grand prince held the land in joint ownership with his boyars, both formally through the higher crown administrators and in actuality through the social authority of major landowners. Even while relying upon the boyars as the pillars of his organizational sway, the grand prince accomplished their utter subjugation to his political will by insistent and often stern measures. Ambiguous and contradictory relationships formed that were punctuated by persistent and angry conflicts.

The concentration of all Great Russian boyars in service at the court of the grand prince generated a sharp numerical growth of this highest stratum of crown servitors. But this development profoundly changed the social composition of the boyar class. Its ancient nucleus was the old boyar group of the Moscow court, which retained its core membership. These boyars were joined by the service princes who descended to the boyar level after losing the last vestiges of their former political independence. Among boyars of formerly independent principalities or the autonomous state of Novgorod, only the fortunate highest ranking persons became part of the upper class of the new capital. The remaining majority "grew lean" as provincial noblemen either subsisting on their own estates or transferred at the harsh command of the Great Russian prince to new duties and lands.

V.O. Kliuchevsky published a tentative account showing that in the sixteenth century hardly forty of 200 boyar families could trace their origins to the old Moscow boyar class of the early fifteenth century. When these 200 boyars are counted as individuals, it appears that only about seventy possessed no noble title. According to Kliuchevsky, this prevalence of titled boyars, or so-called petty princes, exerted a decisive influence in the history of relations between the boyars and the crown. It explains the boyar claims to prestigious and influential roles due descendants of hereditary princes. "Transfer of power was not interrupted," he wrote, "but rather transformed. Power now became collective, with a class and social foundation, and ceased to be isolated, individual and local." At the core of the boyar administrative role in the Muscovite state lay the "continuity of succession extending back to the time of the appanages." This formula, however, did not explain but rather concealed the deeper essence of the historical relationships studied.

The same image of "lord of all the lords of the Russian land" at another time pleased the fancy of the young Tsar Ivan the Terrible, who wrote to the King of Sweden: "Our boyars and governing officials are the children and grandchildren of ancient native grand princes, while others are the children of princes of the Golden Horde, and yet others, brothers of the Polish crown and the grand princedom of Lithuania, or relatives and grandchildren of the grand princedoms of Tver, Riazan, Suzdal and other grand princedoms; they are not commoners." There are no instances where the Moscow autocrats sensed danger from political pretensions based on the former princely grandeur of the noble boyars. The roots of the boyar claims with which the Moscow rulers had to reckon went deeper and were older, as explained by V.O. Kliuchevsky himself in one of the chapters of his study, *The Boyar Council.*[2]

CROWN AND BOYAR RULE

The overall ruling activity of the grand prince long had followed well-defined and customary forms. The most typical of these involved the resolution of legal and administrative questions, such as the functioning of the prince's personal suite within the boyar council. In his "Instructions to His Children," Vladimir Monomakh included in his description of a normal day for the prince the moment for "sitting and contemplating affairs with one's retinue and servitors; having composed his decrees the prince should call his retinue for consultations." This practice survived persistently for centuries, growing and expanding.

Ivan III legislated in the same circumstances as had Monomakh when he created his "Statute on Interest Payments."[3] The Law Code of 1497[4] was legislated by "Grand Prince Ivan Vasilievich, ruler of all Russia, with his children and with the boyars." Similarly, Ivan the Terrible's Law Code stated, concerning new laws: "If there are new matters that are not treated in this law code, those matters shall be reported on by the sovereign and resolved by all the boyars, and then such decision shall be recorded in this law code."

Upon the formation of the vast Great Russian state, the grand princes utilized the ancient customary methods for organizing the central government. They ruled it with the constant participation of the boyar council, which was assembled in one of the court chambers, and consisted either of all the boyars, or of select groups if deliberations concerned specialized questions or more intimate, "privy" political affairs. In the latter instances it was necessary to proceed with some caution in determining whom to call to such a council. Other consultations included the metropolitan and his holy entourage of bishops and abbots, delegations of princes, boyars and clergy, and finally, in matters of special importance, all boyars living on local maintenance and even individuals of secondary service rank throughout the realm, if they were experienced in warfare. Thus did Ivan III in 1471 explain his plan for a major campaign against Novgorod to a massive assembly to which all bishops, princes, boyars, governors and noted soldiers had been invited, representing the entire military might of the grand princedom.

These servitors, with the addition of the prince's clergy, had some reason to consider themselves to be the ruling class. This was an even more reasonable assumption for the higher boyars who were the unfailing participants in all decision-making and actions of the crown government. The question arises as to whether the boyar administrative role was a right or an obligation. First of all, this role was a normal element of their life which dated from the most ancient times. Russian public opinion as expressed in written documents saw the best guarantee of good government in this collaboration between ruling princes and senior boyars experienced in military, legal and civil affairs. Consequently, heavy responsibilities were imposed on the prince's boyars.

Yet the literature of medieval Russia is rich in accusations of boyar advisors for the failures of foreign policy, for petty wars between princes, oppression of the people, and all other shortcomings in the ruling of the state. The princes themselves enjoined their sons to pay heed to senior boyars who wished them well and served them faithfully. On the other hand, young rulers were warned to ignore "evil" counsel when making agreements, and to punish harshly boyar intrigues that might lead to disputes and internecine warfare among princes. It was not by chance that the Moscow chronicler placed in the mouth of Dmitry Donskoi these final words: "And then he said to the boyars: 'With you I ruled the Russian land; with you I took courage on the field of battle and strengthened the grand princedom, defended my patrimony, held cities and great expanses of territory; with you I shared bitterness and joy and I considered you not boyars, but princes of my land.'"

The ancient tradition of close boyar collaboration in all affairs and interests of the prince's government gained particular significance during the organization of the Muscovite state. The policies of the crown introduced an unavoidable complexity into all government activity, creating the need for new measures to accommodate this trend. The reign of Ivan III was an epoch of administrative transformations and of a new legal codification. The law code prepared in 1497 had the fundamental purpose of reforming the primary juridical system of the principality of Moscow. The "court of the grand prince" became a broad ministry controlling all legal matters concerning the secular and clerical privileged landowners, as well as the most important affairs of the population of their lands. Reports from provincial legal jurisdictions also were to be submitted to the central law court.

THE CROWN COURT OF LAW

The "court of the grand prince" was only formally his personal court. The formulation "I, the grand prince, shall judge or delegate the authority to judge" came to mean centralization of numerous crown activities in Moscow, in nascent government departments of a special type. The evolution from the archaic methods of personal princely judgement or thàt of his more or less casual deputies, to more institutionalized forms of jurisprudence, essentially was completed by the Law Code of Ivan the Terrible. It stated: "The law court of the tsar and the grand prince shall judge the provincial and court boyars, as well as other official and crown secretaries." The initial state in re-shaping the grand prince's law court came in the codification of Ivan III: "The court shall judge the boyars and provincial officials, while these shall sit in judgement of [crown] secretaries and lesser officials." A unique form of law court offices evolved, with a definite composition and clear jurisdictional limits. In conception this entire legal system comprised the court of the grand prince, just as the entire crown administration was his "state", directed by boyars appointed by the prince to do his bidding. This held true whether the subject was an area of legal affairs, a region of his realm, or a specific type of governmental problem.

The overall activity of this administration was guided by the exercise of the sovereign's personal power and involvement. He was the source of all authority, the center of all direction and supervision of government activities. The prince's function was to set policies for trusted deputies of grand princely authority and the executors of his will, the boyars. His direction or orders established the procedures of individual commissions of boyars, individual boyars and their assistants, crown secretaries and subordinates. Policies might be temporary or permanent, following decrees that gradually became institutionalized in government departments.

BOYAR ADMINISTRATION AND LAW COURTS

The Muscovite government of princely and boyar rule trod on an evolutionary path leading from antiquated administrative forms toward an elementary structure of state administration that in time would be transformed into a modern bureaucracy. Two centuries were required for the slow development of this new system, but the initial changes can be traced to the time of Ivan III. During his rule the first attempts were made at forming a central government and switching the relationships between the central authority and the regional administrations to a new foundation. The most important role in these attempts at government restructuring, as well as for the eventual and largely unexpected final result in the sixteenth century, was played by the steadfast administrative activity of the boyars, the impoverished servitors of their master, the grand prince.

The need to adapt to the newly emerging administrative system and new manners of government service greatly influenced the boyars' position. Necessarily, a more precise, formal and official definition of the boyar class arose, one which demarcated it more clearly from other strata of the service nobility. In the Law Code of 1497 the term "boyar" attained a unique descriptive and official definition in connection with the concept of the "boyar law court." In regional administration a distinction was made between appointed crown governors who received maintenance in kind locally, together with legal jurisdiction over their charges in a "boyar law court," and those who received such maintenance but without the right to judge their subject populations. Only the former specifically were granted the title of boyar; hence the right to hold court comprised the essential distinction of boyar rank. V.O. Kliuchevsky has attempted to define the boyar court as a body with the right to judge matters concerning the boyars. His approach is extremely labored and succeeds merely in diverting the reader from true understanding of the stipulations of the Law Code of 1497. The commentary of N.I. Lange[5] comes closer to a proper understanding. He equates the boyar law court with the courts held in Moscow by the upper circle of boyars at the court of the grand prince. Actually they were not equivalent, although the boyar court of the Law Code of 1497 is a further development of the court of these high-ranking boyars.

Similarly, the boyar law court cannot be defined successfully by listing the matters within its jurisdiction. Several articles of the Law Code indicate that the boyar court might sit in judgement of all matters, ranging from civil disputes to crimes requiring the death penalty. Its purpose was to adjudicate civil suits involving debts. For many offenses the judging boyar's role was to examine and verify submitted documents, and to uphold actions of lower courts. Hence, the boyar court was apparently an appeals court of the grand prince, hearing appeals and confirming sentences that it might receive from lower judges, that is, from those who received maintenance but did not have the right to convene boyar law courts. Eloquent proof for this definition of the boyar law court is to be found in the fees or tariffs it could claim for its services; they were equal to those of the personal law court of the grand prince. Thus, the boyar court was merely a special form of the central crown court of law.

Such a definition may seem to contradict the existence of the boyar law courts of the appointed crown governors, but it is not by accident that the Law Code places the "boyar right of appeal" of Moscow on the same level as the "governor's appeal" of the provincial cities, namely, as an appeal to a governor or boyar enjoying maintenance with the right to hold a boyar court. This was a feature of the administrative structure of the period when jurisdiction was not vested in impersonal institutions, but originated in personal directives and assignments

of the prince. In sending one of his inner circle or council boyars to be a governor, the grand prince invested in him the authority to conduct boyar courts, the same authority granted to
the boyars commissioned to sit in Moscow. A procedure of this
kind was also customary for medieval governments of Western
Europe.

LIMITATION OF BOYAR AUTHORITY

After a time it was found necessary in the Law Code of Ivan the
Terrible to restrict the authority of the boyar law courts of the
governors as a means of strengthening central institutions. Consequently, understanding of the boyar legal institution was seriously hampered for later investigators, who sought to con-
struct a definition based on features that were typical at an
earlier chronological stage. During the time of Ivan III, however, the scope of authority of the appointed crown governors
was conducive to placement of the higher court in the hands of
trusted persons close to the inner circle of the grand prince, and
to define legal authority more precisely. Appeals were considered and decisions confirmed in the obligatory presence at
the court of jurors, including the elected peasant elders and the
best men of the local peasant communes. Thus the appeals received were assured of proper examination.

Simultaneously the government of the grand prince undertook to confine the duties of governor within clearer legal
boundaries. Broad grants of maintenance were to be limited by
more regulatory restrictions concerning the rights and field of
activities of local officials. This purpose was fulfilled by the
local administrative charters that appeared during the rule of
Ivan III. The concept came from Novgorod. When Grand Prince
Vasily Dmitrievich[6] temporarily seized a district of Novgorod
the Great the people were persuaded to submit to the grand
prince by a special charter obliging the appointed officials to
proceed judiciously in their legal and policing endeavors and in

collecting taxes. One such administrative charter, granted to the populace of the Dvina land, was intended to protect them from arbitrary acts by the local appointed officials by imposing elementary legal procedures on the latter.

When Ivan III forced Novgorod to rescind its treaty relationships with the grand prince's government, he refused the city's petitions for a similar charter that would protect the people by determining the taxable assets that the appointed crown governors could claim for administrative needs. Later, however, Ivan himself and his successors followed the practice of granting to local populations administrative charters limiting the scope of activities and the arbitrary acts of appointed officials.

The sum total of these structural innovations in crown administration placed the executive organs of government on a new operational foundation. Their personnel were faced with reeducation in the spirit of responsible government, functioning as agents of the highest crown authority and obedient tools of the will of their sovereign. Their authorized powers lost the stamp of independence and became merely manifestations of the unified supreme power functioning through subordinate administrative institutions. But there did not yet exist the power, the resources or the organizational acumen for establishing a proper bureaucracy. As a result, a complex system of relationships emerged, based on adaptations to the tasks and forms of the structure of the state; this system lent strength to the boyar class, which long had supported and assisted the grand prince's activities. The basic feature of this adaptation was the more definite and specific differentiation of the grand prince's servitors into the so-called Moscow estates.

THE SERVICE HIERARCHY

Of truly great importance in this process was the stream of new gentry into the ranks of the boyars, including landholders of patrimonial principalities and other members of the aristocracy.

The former narrow circle of close servitors of the grand prince therefore expanded greatly and assumed a different social hue. It is difficult to determine the position of service princes among the Moscow boyars. The solution to this problem was begun during the era of Ivan III and Vasily III by devising a system for calculating ranks. Kliuchevsky provided the very astute insight that the roots of regulation of position in the service hierarchy should be sought in the princely rather than the boyar tradition.[7] The basic foundation of this system comes from the principle of brotherly equality among princes, with a senior prince at the head. In agreements between princes there are precise conditions stating that certain of them will join in military campaigns only if the grand prince heads the army host, while other military forces are led by his sons. Should a boyar replace him as military leader, the other independent princes would also send their troops under the command of military leaders.

The grand princes sought to elevate their military authority above these placement considerations, and in part they succeeded. Nevertheless, such concepts and customs sent down deep roots into the service nobility. In relation to service to the grand prince, this tradition took on particularly keen significance as a guarantee of the high official and social position of the aristocracy. In several respects princely servitors remained the ruling princes that they had been. Their military forces and fortified estates held special positions in the army of the grand prince, remaining under the direct command of the prince himself and separate from the general order of battle of the Muscovite army. The princely servitors took their places alongside the troops of Moscow according to their fancy rather than according to an imposed plan. Only toward the end of Ivan III's reign did the service princes begin to appear as military leaders subordinate to an appointed commander-in-chief and at the head of the regiments of Moscow. They still remained apart from the Moscow boyars.

The same situation observed by Kliuchevsky in military organization held also for the grand prince's council. The grand
prince consulted with the princes and boyars, and these two
groups continued to retain their distinct features and genealogical foundations for some time. Entry of the princes into the
service of the grand prince unavoidably affected the position
of the boyars, whose social composition underwent a process
of stratification. The individuals at the pinnacle of the ancient
Moscow boyar class successfully defended their proximate positions to the grand prince, according to the particular importance of their land holdings. Yet there were factors in the composition of the group of voluntary servitors of boyar origins
which gradually brought the descent of the Moscow boyars into the second stratum at the prince's court. The official terminology of the period preserved certain curious features of the
transition. A portion of the grand prince's retinue at court,
having descended in the aristocracy, came to be called lesser
boyars while nonetheless retaining the positions of boyars in
the prince's service. This is the proper understanding of the
lesser boyars, a term which describes individuals holding maintenance and the right to boyar law courts as delineated in the
Law Code of 1497 (even though in the tsar's Law Code this
was already an antiquated feature), and "those lesser boyars
who live in council with the sovereign." There is no basis for
seeing this group as something new, a product of the anti-boyar
policies of the crown government. Nor should such an interpretation be given to the council secretaries, those descendants of
the former privy secretaries, or other highly-placed crown secretaries of bygone days.

Ancient coteries within the grand prince's court and council had been reduced to secondary positions by the flood of
aristocratic newcomers. Yet they had not lost their importance.
The highest ranking princes and boyars stood at the crest of
Moscow court society. More properly, they should be placed
at its head, since they did not consider themselves to be, nor

were they called, the courtiers of the sovereign grand prince. That appellation came into usage only gradually, after long ambiguity, as the term applying to a lower echelon of former servitors or lesser boyars. The distinction between the lesser boyars of the grand prince's court, and his common courtiers, was preserved for a long period. Throughout this restructuring, a struggle continued between divergent tendencies arising, on one hand, from factors of service and proximity to crown authority, and on the other, from the aristocratic social position that the servitor had inherited from his ancestors.

GENEALOGY AND SERVICE

For the highest aristocracy this battle ended with the establishment of the service hierarchy with its two contradictory principles of genealogy and rank. The position of a boyar at official court functions was to be determined by those placed above, alongside and below him according to the relative venerability of his ancestry. His service rank had no role in determining this position. A boyar might perform a duty above or below his station in the hierarchy as long as the service relationship in no way violated the hierarchical placements. The determinations yielded by this system illuminated the service character of boyar aristocracy with special brilliance. Notwithstanding ancestry, the aristocracy of boyars and princes was defined through the books of ranks bestowed by the grand prince, as well as by genealogy. Consequently, advancement in the grand prince's service had a positive effect in improving one's place in the hierarchy, while without such achievement a noble might decline in aristocratic importance.

Without a doubt the hierarchy of aristocracy contained a political meaning. It connected the supreme will of the autocratic sovereign to several inflexible standards that he was obliged to observe in utilizing his service nobility. Likewise, it bound him in matters of counsel. The concept of councillor to the grand prince is closely associated with the boyars. Although the palace boyars[8] were replaced by those of the boyar council,[9] in fact this was more a change in terminology than in practice. On the other hand, the customs imposed by the hierarchical system placed a particular limitation on newly-appointed boyars, as they had on the former privy boyars. The grand prince was compelled to reckon with the genealogy of the boyars in conferring the rank of councillor on them. The broadening of the membership of the boyar council was achieved by bestowing the rank of councillor on provincial boyars as secondary members of this class; through this practice there evolved a rank through which a boyar of minor importance must pass to attain significant standing at court. The boyar families situated lower in the aristocratic hierarchy did not rise higher than the rank of councillor. The circle of boyar councillors also was expanded by the inclusion of lesser boyars in the state council,[10] and of the grand prince's prestigious crown secretaries in the council. Yet together the procedures merely modified the aristocratic character of the boyar council, without removing the inherent contradiction which lay at the core of that institution. It was an institution of high authority, striving to gain unlimited autocratic power, yet it was formed not of persons freely selected by the sovereign grand prince, but with his sufferance in observance of common law practices and the claims of the highest-ranking among his aristocratic servitors.

The significance in government of the boyar council was bound to grow mightily during a period when the aims and activities of the administration swelled in fundamental and powerful ways in stride with the formation of the vast Great Russian state. The boyar decrees were the usual form of official and legal executive activity of the crown, while legal deliberations "with his boyars" comprised the normal basis of the activity of the grand prince's law court. In council with his boyars and princes, the grand prince conducted foreign policy, negotiations with foreign states, and the preparation and abrogation of treaties.

With all its multifarious functions, did the boyar council have an independent political significance? Doubtless it had such significance in the social consciousness of Muscovite Russia, but for a true characterization and evaluation any formal, legalistic or "constitutional" approach must be abandoned. From such a viewpoint, the boyar council in no way limited the power of the sovereign. On the contrary, it executed in traditional ways the undertakings of the sovereign's government, and upheld the traditional common law perceptions shared by society as a whole, as well as by the legal and political administration. The preservation of the ancient customs and traditions that constituted the usual order of things, and of rights recognized from time beyond reckoning, was regarded as the ideal charge of the prince's advisors. The very service of the boyars by sword as well as by counsel had been an essential element of those ancient customs and traditions. The grand prince's lust for unlimited autocracy both in practice and in principle introduced discord into the traditional relationships and undermined the very concept of the unbreakable bond between the ruler and the traditions of the distant past.

Organizational problems of horrendous difficulty confronted the government of the Muscovite state. Having just consolidated its rule over Great Russia, Moscow sought to create a large and dependable military force, to establish a state financial system, and to coordinate the exploitation of the entire might and resources of the country. The inadequacy of these resources in relation to the rapidly growing activities of the crown was felt at every step. Such an undertaking called for a powerful and closely centralized government. The struggle to establish such a government was tense and erratic; it constituted the fundamental feature of Muscovy's domestic politics. Functioning in the given conditions of a hereditary land structure which shaped the political beliefs of the period, and imbued with the urge to gather into its hands the reins of power scattered among the hereditary lands, the autocracy of Moscow gradually emerged and in so doing crushed common traditions and out-dated legal principles.

CROWN AND BOYAR

With its very first steps down the path of history the Muscovite autocracy collided with the conservative inertia of the boyar class. Moscow's striving to erect an autocratic order conflicted with the venerated social notions of legal guarantees to preserve the ancient customs and traditions in all spheres of law and administration. In such circumstances the most violent conflicts between the sovereigns of Muscovy and the boyars always were played out in relation to the limits on power imposed by common-law traditions, as opposed to the credo of unlimited autocratic freedom.

During the reign of Ivan III only one instance of harsh reprisal is known. The grand prince, reacting to the "haughtiness" of the boyars, executed a certain Starodubsky-Riapolovsky and forced the Patrikeevs, father and son, to enter a monastery. S.M. Soloviev convincingly and painstakingly demonstrated the relationship between that violence and the battle in the court over succession, namely whether the grandson Dmitry or the son Vasily would follow Ivan Vasilievich to the throne. This affair was mentioned previously. The boyar princes insisted on the right of Dmitry, as the first-born of the co-ruler, Grand Prince Ivan Ivanovich, to succeed to power, while Ivan III supported his son by Tsarina Sofia. In this Ivan III was supported by the lesser courtiers, the lesser boyars and the non-aristocratic crown secretaries. During this conflict Grand Prince Ivan adamantly proclaimed his total freedom to guide the affairs of state according to his autocratic whim.

An enduring court tradition grew up in connection with the name and influence of Sofia Paleologus who inspired discord

at the grand prince's court, which undermined ancient customs
and alienated the sovereign from his boyar councillors. Members of the boyar council began to whisper of the grand prince's
haughtiness, of his estrangement from boyar society and how
he exalted himself above them as the sovereign of the realm.
He was arranging the affairs of the realm without consulting
the boyar council, and relying upon the private advice of his
trusted favorites. His failure to seek advice and counsel caused
the sovereign to be severely reproached. The words for which
Grand Prince Vasily III executed the young boyar council
member Bersen-Beklemishev were reechoed in the letters of
Prince Andrei Kurbsky,[11] who condemned Ivan the Terrible
for failure to hark to the boyar council's recommendations.
The sovereign's arbitrary decisions and personal rule drew protest and gained him reproach for his unilateral decisions, personal rule, haughtiness and pride, reported the anonymous
author of a commentary to the work *Discourse of the Miracle-
Workers of Valaam.*[12] This criticism was motivated, as Kurbsky
put it, by the notion that if the tsar were honest in his rule
but had not "received the gifts from God" needed for governing, he should seek good and useful advice. The basic premise
here was the avoidance of arbitrary personal rule, a considera-
tion which went beyond the preservation of the importance of
the boyar council. In the writings of the two authors mentioned
criticism became instruction in the usefulness of counsel not
merely of special advisors, but from the entire people; not
only the advice of wise and dependable leaders close to the
ruler, but universal counsel solicited from all the towns and
their districts.

A particularly bitter aspect of the dispute between the tsar's
government and the boyars, which provoked mutual accusations of haughtiness, originated at the time of Ivan III in the
personal law court of the grand prince. The personal right to
sit in punitive judgement had belonged to the princes for centuries and it was not accidental that the bishops instilled in

Saint Vladimir[13] the idea that he was "ordained by God to punish evil men and to have mercy on the just." Yet those very bishops went on to explain that the prince, of course, should practice all due process in punishing criminals. This came to mean, in the grand prince's dispensation of justice, that he should sit with his boyars to determine judgements, with the boyar council. The crown law court followed common-law procedures. Just as for the court of the "grand prince's children" and the boyar law court, the Law Code of 1497 established the fee structure for this court. Ivan III moved forcefully to replace these inhibiting formalities in his higher legal system by claiming the right to impose his own penalties and to seize property in violation of established legal procedures. He proclaimed his right of immunity to decisions of a court of justice which included his boyars. Almost immediately the boyars protested against sentences handed down without court hearings, as in the case of Prince Obolensky-Lyk, who was condemned without formal legal proceedings.

THE AGREEMENT OF 1565

During the time of Ivan the Terrible the dispute over the proper court procedures applicable to the tsar and grand prince, in contrast to arbitrary rule by edict, gathered particular force and heat. The argument culminated in a sort of agreement between tsar and people in 1565. Ivan had left the capital for the suburb of Aleksandrovsk, threatening to abandon the realm entirely. He voiced a sweeping denunciation of the clergy, boyars, officials and servitors because, in his words, they all had connived to shield from the tsar's wrath those he wished to punish for their crimes. All who supposedly had supported the sovereign in his rule in actuality were guilty of undermining his power. The petition received in reply from the influential people and all of Muscovy implored that the sovereign should not desert his realm, and that his sovereign will should be done in punishing violators of the common welfare. Tsar Ivan agreed to reassume his rule on condition that he might banish all traitors and insubordinates, or execute them and confiscate their property. Therewith disappeared at once two customs which had restrained the arbitrary will of the supreme ruler in matters of law and punishment. No longer might the clergy intervene on behalf of the banished, and no longer might the customary practices of the highest court prevail. Imposing moral and formal obstacles to the autocrat's arbitrary exercise of his will concerning the person and property of his subjects now fell by the wayside.

In essence, the tsar acquired no new authority in 1565. As Baron Herberstein wrote about Vasily III, the sovereign "applied his power to the clergy as well as to the laity, disposed without restraint and at his will with the lives and property of all." Yet Ivan the Terrible, by turn of mind a strict interpreter of the written word, was by nature a demanding and extremely self-centered despot. He sought to escape any formal limitations whatsoever on his power, and to shape the public opinion of his time in order to achieve unconditional subordination based on both fear and conscience. He wanted complete and submissive acceptance of his actions, renunciation of the slightest right to censure him, and removal of every formal and moral restraint on his most extreme expressions of autocratic will. He had assimilated thoroughly those conceptions of tsarist power that had so struck Baron Herberstein in the court milieu of Grand Prince Vasily III. The foreign observer noted with amazement that the Russians openly regarded the will of the sovereign to be the will of God, and believed that all the acts of their ruler were executed according to the will of God, since in all things the tsar merely served as the instrument of divine guidance. Hence, Herberstein continued, it was no wonder that if you asked a Russian about some doubtful or inexplicable phenomenon, he would answer: "Only God and the tsar know about that."

THE ANNOINTED OF GOD

The personal might of the tsar as the annointed of God ascended to a height unapproached by all worldly rights and any mortal truth. The fundamental idea of autocracy lay in recognizing the higher authority and will of the sovereign as the source and ultimate criterium of all right and justice. This view contains the essence of the unique mystique of autocracy proclaimed by apologists of Russian absolutism, which was expressed with consummate brilliance in the seventeenth century by Ivan the Terrible's devotee, Tsar Alexis Mikhailovich.[14] Tsar Alexis believed in the tsar's holy origin and in the direct divine guidance of the tsar's will. Hence he demanded of his subjects not merely sincere service, but "joyful obedience," and denounced those who did not devote themselves to the tsar with all their hearts. Thereby Alexis placed the tsar's mercy higher than any right and reduced personal and private rights to submission to the supreme discretion of the sovereign.

In the nineteenth century this same idea was resurrected with new vitality in the official theory of Nicholas I's absolutism. Supreme authority, as the tool of Providence, was analogous in public life to the role of private conscience as guided by religion in the daily rounds of life. The theory of unconditional power evolved into the dogma of unconditional governmental authority. The deep principles of Eastern caesaropapism lay buried at the base of this evolution, forming the pillars upholding the actual practices of autocracy. Accordingly Ivan the Terrible recognized the responsibility of the mighty tsar before God to protect the purity of the faith in his subject people; secular power was summoned to guide the religious and moral life of the populace.

AUTOCRACY AND OPPOSITION

Meanwhile destructive storms of executions and debauchery at court were thundering over Muscovite Russia, destroying everyday traditions and principles. The sway of Ivan the Terrible's bodyguards known as the oprichnina[15] was responsible for this situation. Then like a sea swell it receded, poisoning in its ebbing the reign of Boris Godunov with suspicions, hidden enmity, secret investigations and arbitrary despotism. The public conscience was not moved by the open display of such power, but rather stagnated in a "senseless silence throughout the whole world," in the words of a perceptive contemporary. When once again boyar society regained the opportunity to raise its voice, it spoke of legal guarantees of personal and property immunity from arbitrary whims of the tsar's punitive authority. The boyar tsar, Vasily Shuisky, pledged in a special oath on the cross not to execute anyone, or to confiscate anyone's property, without seeking the counsel of his boyars.

The attempt to resist the excesses of the tsar's autocracy through the conservative boyar council constituted the basic tactics of the boyar opposition during the sixteenth century. This was the essential meaning of the council, inseparably linked to the boyars' service as advisors and to the impact on law of measures favored by the boyars. Yet this congery of concepts and aspirations contained no suggestions advanced by the provincial administrators whatsoever. Its basis was older, broader and deeper, and it must be sought in the ancient heritage of the limitation of princely authority by common-law customs and traditions. At the head of the opposition to the tsar's autocracy stood, primarily, the representatives of the titled boyar class. Their aim was not to shield the ambitions of the hereditary provincial landholders, but to advance the cause of the boyar opposition, and in a broader sense, to preserve the customs of the land. Active in parallel with this concern to safeguard the established ways was the urge of self-interest native to this patrimonial and aristocratic class. The process of strengthening the tsar's authority forced a wedge between the interests of the boyars and the sovereign, who then found new popular support in the less aristocratic elements of society. The introduction of new principles of military service and taxation crushed utterly the presumptuous privileged servitors and landholders. The first to fall were the descendants of the former reigning princes, who were followed in destruction by the entire noble boyar class. The survival of the established legal customs of the land had become intertwined with the cause of boyar privileges, and both succumbed under the blows of the autocracy. The tsar discovered a mighty tower of support in the Russian middle classes, who were hostile to the boyars. For the most part these were the everyday officials and the local office holders. Relying on them, the militant, powerful autocracy was able to maneuver freely against the boyars and the entire range of the accepted customs of the land.[16]

CHAPTER SIX

CHURCH AND STATE IN MUSCOVY

CLERGY AND HIERARCHY

The "sovereign's clergy" stood next to the princes and boyars
in close proximity to the grand prince's government. In ancient
Russia the church was a powerful social and political force, and
the Russian metropolitanate as part of the patriarchate of Constantinople maintained inviolable bonds outside Russia to a
higher center of church governance, the "universal" patriarch
of Byzantium. As a matter of course the patriarch appointed
a prominent Byzantine cleric to be the head of the native Russian clergy. This cultivated clergyman, armed with sweeping authority, would appear in a country that to sophisticated Byzantium appeared barbarian, bringing with him a higher culture
and a superior spiritual authority that was independent of local
rulers. This organizational basis of the Russian hierarchy endowed it with considerable latitude in the world of Russian
politics. The independent position of the Russian metropolitanate among the domestic political forces contributed to the
divisions and fragmentation of the grand prince's political sov-
ereignty. In the fourteenth and fifteenth centuries the division
of the Russian lands between two mighty political competitors,
the Russo-Lithuanian state and the Great Russian grand principality, immensely complicated the position of the church. The
transfer of the metropolitan's residence from Kiev to Vladimir,
in the Great Russian North, bound the metropolitanate more
closely to Great Russia's affairs and interests. The seat at Vladimir of the metropolitan of all Russia gathered around it the
groups in society that were suffering the upheavals of disinte-
grating political relations as the small patrimonial principalities gradually declined in land and power. In this political

configuration the boyars of the grand prince and the native clergy, together with the metropolitanate, began their decline.

During the first years of the fourteenth century, when Metropolitan Maxim was setting the precedent of maintaining his residence in Vladimir, a remarkable literary monument appeared. It was a comprehensive chronicle that included all the Russian lands in its scope but focused on and relied on the local records of events in northern, southern and western Russia. With the support of Metropolitan Maxim, these local developments inspired the prince of Tver, Michael Yaroslavich, to adopt the title grand prince of all Russia and to make an unsuccessful but significant attempt to subordinate all Russia to a single and more mighty authority, led by the grand prince. Maxim's immediate successors, Peter, a native of southern Russia, and the Greek Theognostus, adopted the whole of this Great Russian political idea. After Michael's failure, with the boyars of the grand prince they hurried from Tver to Moscow in search of the long-sought firm center for a new attempt at unification. The church hierarchy now directed its pastoral influence toward the support of the ambitions of Moscow's princes as a means of strengthening the authority of the grand prince.

METROPOLITAN ALEXIS [1354-1378]

Under these conditions the process of nationalizing the Russian church intensified. Theognostus' successor to the metropolitan's seat looms as an imposing political figure who ascended to this office from among the boyars of the grand prince's court. As it turned out, Alexis became not merely the head of the church but the shepherd of political life in Great Russia as well. Unlike his predecessors, he compelled the highest members of the church hierarchy to serve secular political aims more openly and consistently than heretofore. The church now defended the pretensions of the grand prince of Moscow to rule throughout Great Russia, and assisted in strengthening his power

over other ruling princes in northern Russia as well as in the
continuing battle with Lithuania for the western regions of the
realm. The ruler-metropolitan, Alexis, introduced a clearly defined Orthodox religious, and thereby nationalistic, ideology
into Great Russian politics. In a lively correspondence with
Constantinople and in his pastoral admonitions to Russian
princes, Metropolitan Alexis nurtured the concept that Orthodox Russia was a part of the holy Christian community that
formed the political body of the church, while the government
of the grand prince of all Russia and the authority of the Russian metropolitan safeguarded the church. This doctrine lay be-
hind the idea that Moscow's struggle with "heathen" Lithuania,
led by the "fire-worshipper" Olgerd,[1] warranted the sympathy
and support of the entire Christian world. Similar justification
was cited for the demand that the Russian princes maintain
unity with the grand prince, pledged by kissing the cross, and
that they serve his cause with their military might, under penalty of excommunication by both patriarch and metropolitan.

Metropolitan Alexis' policy stressed the Great Russian character of the metropolitanate and sought to transform the Russian church into an institution of the Great Russian state. In
fact, however, he held authority over "Kiev and all Russia."
The national and Great Russian emphasis in his activities lent
to his ecclesiastic administration a biased political orientation
in relations with the Russian eparchies of the Russo-Lithuanian
state. The metropolitanate found itself at a hopeless juncture,
and a division into separate Great Russian and Western Russian
groups became inevitable. Grand Prince Dmitry Donskoi turned
in that direction upon the death of Alexis, hoping only to retain the right to appoint the candidate for the office of metropolitan; Dmitry also wished to preserve church influence as an
active force in the grand prince's politics.

Nevertheless, a significant segment of the clergy revered the
ancient unity of the metropolitanate. Its political weight was
responsible for Moscow's influence on Orthodox areas of

Western Russia. These areas were vacillating between Moscow and Lithuania, where they sought support against Moscow's domination. The prolonged discord within the church revolved primarily around the claims of the grand prince of Moscow to select the metropolitan, and the problem of church unity. It ended in the complete victory of the partisans of unity and independence of the authority of the grand prince. Metropolitans Kiprian from Bulgaria and Photius of Greece abandoned the doctrines instituted by Alexis by separating their policies from those of the secular government. They adopted the posture of metropolitans of all Russia who led the church with the support of their ecclesiastic superior, the patriarch of Constantinople. Meanwhile, in secular matters they searched for an accommodating middle way that would maintain cordial relations with both Great Russia and Lithuania. For the moment, Moscow had lost a major pillar of support for its claim to power. On the other hand, the metropolitanate in those years very strongly defended its secular interests and pastoral authority. The grand prince himself was to bow to the metropolitan of all Russia as a spiritual son of his father.

CHURCH ESTATES

The subordination of the metropolitanate and the entire church hierarchy to the grand prince held tremendous importance for the latter in relations between princes and with foreign states. The church possessed enormous secular influence thanks to the extensive landholdings of monasteries and other church institutions, and to their unique economic role as holders of relatively large amounts of money. A reasonable estimate of the extent of church landholdings is impossible. There is a foreign report from the mid-sixteenth century stating that, after what can be presumed to have been a period of relative stability, monasteries controlled as much as one third of all the lands of Muscovite Russia. This eyewitness estimate may well have been

greatly exaggerated, perhaps even with calculated intention, by
the informants among the Muscovite boyars who provided information to Captain Chancellor, who in turn passed his information on to Clement Adams, the author of the story of
distant Muscovy.[2] Yet when several conditions favorable to
the development of such agricultural wealth are recalled, including the large land grants made by princes and other hereditary landlords, perhaps the exaggeration is not great. The monasteries displayed much energy in their economic endeavors,
and became the first capitalistic element in Russia. They received broad financial exemptions and grants, and in time their
land holdings evoked the deep concern of the Moscow authorities as well as, during the reign of Ivan III, of the prince's secular servitors. At the same time, Chancellor's report must be
measured against the accepted estimate of the extent of church
estates in Western Europe in the late medieval period, according to which in many countries one fifth, one fourth, and even
one third of all land belonged to the church. In consequence,
the estimate for Russia may not be so exaggerated after all.
Together with the monastic lands must be numbered the holdings of various bishoprics and, especially, the immense estates
of the metropolitanate itself.

The position of the lands held by religious institutions within Great Russia was basically comparable to the landholdings
of the princes and boyars within the grand principality. Hereditary rights were vested in individual church institutions whose
superiors functioned in every respect as civil lords. Of the
church lands, the estates belonging to the metropolitanate were
unusually numerous. The charters and decrees assuring the
rights and property of the metropolitanate applied solely to
these lands. Other clerical hereditary landlords, bishops and
abbots enjoyed individual rights, guarantees and charters assuring them of direct links to the crown administration equal to
those of the great secular landowners.

The metropolitan himself stood out in a particular way. During the tenure of Kiprian, the grand prince and the metropolitan jointly determined the place of the metropolitanate in a protocol to their agreement. The terms of the document were close to the arrangements made between the grand prince and the appanage princes. The charter of 1392 warranted the autonomy of the metropolitan's court of law and administration, and set down the obligations and terms of payment applicable to the inhabitants of districts subject to the metropolitanate in accordance with accepted customs and traditions. It pledged the discontinuance of all new practices. Consequently, the sum collected was to be sufficient to pay the tribute to the Tatars according to the established quitrent schedules[3] established by ancient grants. The prince waived even these contributions in years when no tribute was due to the Tatars. The boyars and subjects of the metropolitan marched on campaigns under their own commanders only if the grand prince himself rode at the head of the amassed host of his realm. The basic charter also contained guarantees of immunity for monastic lands. The grand prince was enjoined from sending his agents into the villages of monastery estates for any cause whatsoever, and from passing judgements on their inhabitants. The abbots were to investigate and sit in judgement of all disturbances. If joint law court sessions were held, the proceeds of litigation were to be divided equally between the crown and monastic judges.

These guarantees were not, however, an attempt to safeguard the hereditary privileges of the church. They related only to monasteries defined as belonging in perpetuity to the metropolitanate. Individual bishops and princes also held their "own" monasteries. Together with many secondary ones, the most prestigious monasteries sought direct ties with the supreme secular ruler. While observing the metropolitan's jurisdiction and authority in ecclesiastical matters, these monasteries, even during the zenith of independence of the Russian metropolitanate, stood in immediate subordination to the grand prince in hereditary land ownership and legal responsibility. No other institution could claim to govern abbots, monks and other monastery subjects. Grant charters which established exemptions from patrimonial taxes for the populace and the authority of the abbot over the lands also spelled out the bond of the monastic lands to the crown, and defined the nature of the grand prince's grant. Politically, the grand prince's control over church institutions outside the lands of the metropolitanate was closer and more effective than was the authority of the head of the Russian church. Thus it was natural that the grand prince appeared in the role of defender of Muscovy's churches and monasteries from the metropolitan's assessments and fees. The monasteries with their extensive hereditary lands received special care. Their administration grew ever more closely attached to the court of the grand prince, until by the sixteenth century it had become one of the most important functions of the Chancellery of the Royal Household.[4]

CROWN AND CLERICAL AUTHORITY

In such circumstances it is no wonder that the appointment of abbots, particularly for the more important monasteries, was a matter of great weight for the grand prince. For all practical purposes, he exercised personal supervision of this function. The actual erection of new monasteries usually took place with the direct participation of crown authorities, at least in the sense that emerging monasteries, upon embarking on their activities and building quarters, hastened to obtain grant charters to their fields and forests. They also sought the right to populate their estates with free settlers exempted from state fees, and to be released from the jurisdiction of local authorities in favor of direct subordination to the central crown courts.

Another significant relationship involved the dependence of the diocesan clergy on the grand prince. The medieval Russian eparchy was not purely a spiritual institution; it was also

an administrative and governing institution. The ecclesiastical
hierarchy was organized along secular lines which governed the
relationships of superior and subordinates among the monks
and the parish clergy.[5] The church chancellery stood as the
central hierarchical institution. It dealt with suits and disputes
involving the regular clergy, who were obligated to meet the
direct taxes and quitrents owed from church lands. The administrative head was responsible also for supervising the monasteries, and extensive hereditary estates and their populations,
belonging to the metropolitanate. An entire corps of secular officials and clerks, deputies, courtiers, servants, tithe collectors
and other minor employees were occupied in seeing to the affairs of this church administration. Elements of diocesan and
hereditary administration typically were mingled and inter-
wined, in the pervasive authoritarian spirit of the era. Because
the church administrative structure resembled that of the crown,
church officials increasingly resembled the appointed boyar officials and hereditary landholders in accordance with their role
in the social and political life of Great Russia. The bishops and
abbots, as crown clergy, were drawn to the prince's court. In
rank they were equal to the boyars. The clerics also were involved deeply in court political activities; as the formation of a
unified Great Russia state evolved, more and more they joined
all high-ranking public figures in attendance at the court of the
sovereign grand prince.

The subordination of the church to the crown was deeply
grounded in the overall structure of old Russian society. Domestic and foreign political interests, which contributed to the
evolution toward absolute autocracy, insistently demanded the
comprehensive mobilization of all resources. The transformation of the metropolitanate in Great Russia into an institution
of the Muscovite state became an essential feature of the creative labors of the grand princes of Moscow.

The reign of Vasily the Dark witnessed vicious and bloody
disorders that brought down the last vestiges of the appanage

system. After the crisis was overcome, Muscovite Russia succeeded in establishing the powerful principality inherited by Ivan III, and at the same time abolished the independent and self-sufficient character of the metropolitanate. When Photius died in 1431, a Russian candidate, Bishop Iona, was proposed. The political pressures then being experienced by the Byzantime Empire, whose influence was ebbing as the Turks advanced, led to the candidacy of Metropolitan Isidor, who journied to Russia from Greece. However, at the Council of Florence in 1439 he sided with the proponents of union with Rome. Isidor's travel to Italy, his return, dismissal, and flight postponed the final resolution of the fate of the Russian church for a number of years.

CROWN APPOINTMENT OF METROPOLITANS

At the end of 1448 Moscow decided to place Iona at the head of the metropolitanate through his selection by a council of Great Russian bishops, even at the price of severing ties with the patriarch at Constantinople. Iona followed and completed the work of Peter and Alexis and, in the footsteps of those holy men, became the third Muscovite metropolitan to be raised to sainthood. The canonization of the churchmen by the Muscovite church sanctified as well the metropolitanate's Great Russian nationalism.

From this moment forward, to the dismay of strict local clergymen, metropolitans took office without seeking the blessing of the patriarch in Constantinople. It was not long until the appointment of new bishops included in their charge of office a promise not to accept Byzantine candidates. Henceforth the head of the Muscovite church was selected formally either by the blessing of the previous metropolitan, as Iona consecrated Theodosius, and Theodosius blessed Philip, or by the selection of a candidate at a council of bishops. The latter procedure was in fact the choice of the sovereign grand prince, who raised his candidate to the metropolitanate upon his proclamation and appointment by a council of bishops. The Great Russian metropolitanate now stood in the tsar's presence shorn of all outside support, and thereby became an institution of the Muscovite state. The church remained an influential institution, but a servant of the grand prince's will nonetheless. It tended to its parochial interests and served the needs of the Muscovite state under the mighty hand of the sovereign grand prince, its patron and master. This subjugation of the metropolitanate to civil authority completed the transformation of the Russian church into a dependency of secular rule. The supreme ruler of Great Russia, having assumed the title of tsar, had achieved the same relationship to the church that existed within Eastern Orthodoxy in Byzantium.

The sovereign of Muscovy desired to master the destiny of the church in order to satisfy a number of essential interests and relationships. The edifice of the hereditary Muscovite state included church institutions whose public importance and power were too great to allow the civil authorities to settle the question of church relations in any other manner. The cooperation of monastery and episcopal land holders, the expansion and institutionalization of privileges related to them, and the cultivation of the metropolitan's influence, long had served as underpinnings of the growth of the grand prince's power, in parallel with the other pillars on which rested this expansion, the boyar landholders and servitors. But the second half of the fifteenth century witnessed a rapid and fundamental restructuring of these ties. The grand prince of Muscovy became the hereditary sovereign of the entire Great Russian realm and enjoyed autocratic sway over its men and resources. He began the difficult and complex task of guiding his charges toward the satisfaction of the needs of his state. In smashing the privileges and autonomy of his free servitors, he converted them into crown chattels without major upheavals.

RUSSIAN CAESAROPAPISM

No less a challenge confronted the prince in his relations with the ecclesiastical magnates. There the touchstone was not the liberty of a powerful and influential social stratum, but the ancient financial privileges of the established church and the principles of religious independence and immunity. The power of Moscow's rulers permeated the church clad in the vestments of the tsar, for the ideology implanted in Russian soil by Metropolitan Alexis sanctified and deepened the church's subjugation to the secular ruler. The Byzantine idea thus transplanted to Russia held that the tsar, in formulating the holy Christian policies of the government, inherently required dominion over the church hierarchy. The Byzantines instructed their Russian pupils: "It is impossible for Christians to have a church without also having a tsar, for the empire and the church are indivisibly united and bound to each; it is impossible to separate one from the other." The tsardom of Muscovy received the Byzantine legacy as the latter was retreating before the onslaught of the Turks; consequently, Moscow laid claim to the title of "the Third Rome,"[6] the Orthodox empire that was one with the whole universe. The tsar was the supreme ruler of both church and state. The claim to church authority went no further or deeper than the ideal of the sanctified state in which the tsar's government, the guardian of the canons and of orthodoxy, is informed by religious and ecclesiastical doctrines throughout its ruling and civil functions and in relations between church and state. This meant a great deal, for thereby the power of the crown was confined by moral and religious standards and canonical doctrines interpreted by the church hierarchy. The pastoral obligation of the clergy included intercession with the tsar on behalf of the suffering and injured, his instruction in the proper understanding of good and truth, and condemnation of his sinful and unjust acts. Correspondingly, the tsar as a Christian was obliged to heed such injunctions and to accept them without protest.

Endowed with power bestowed by God yet tempered by mercy and judgement, the tsar was obliged to act on all matters concerning the church, the monasteries, and all of Christendom. The membership of the church hierarchy was determined by the supreme will of the sovereign; by his command church councils were convened, and he set their agenda, took active part in their deliberations, and endorsed their decisions in confirmation of their validity. Without his consent not a single issue of church discipline, worship, or other important or insignificant principle or secondary religious question might be resolved. Inasmuch as the church had vital interests in all these matters, the personal desires and concepts of the sovereign acquired crucial and constant importance for the church.

Where the social and material interests of church institutions conflicted with the goals and aspirations of the crown, bright clashes flared. Essential and vital as such disputes became, they posed with great clarity the fundamental question of harmonizing church authority with the hereditary autocracy whose power was unlimited by any standards of behavior. The inherent insolubility of this problem stamped its seal on the fate of the church in the tsardom of Muscovy.

CHAPTER SEVEN

LAND TENURE

PATRIMONIAL LAND TENURE

Having seized each rein of power, the grand prince of Muscovy resolutely began to organize a military power that would stand immediately and directly at his call. The crushing of independent political power in the regions outside Moscow took on the nature of conquest during the time of Ivan III. Even in circumstances where no military action was involved the new ruler treated the subjected areas as defeated lands. The rights, guarantees and assurances granted to the subject population in earlier acts and charters were nullified or modified with the explanation that such charters had not been granted by the grand princes themselves, but merely by the local authorities. In the troubled years of Vasily the Dark the appanage princes were struggling for their ancestral holdings. They insisted that when inherited lands had been retaken from foreign invaders, an appanage prince need not honor grant charters or purchase deeds issued by the defeated enemy. This demand represented the further development of a general principle of the appanage hereditary structure by which the rights of princes and boyars to manorial holdings in the territories of other princedoms required special permission in each instance from the local government.

The rulers of Novgorod conscientiously and broadly advanced this right in their treaties with the grand princes, insisting on annulment of conflicting purchase agreements or other means of acquisition. In treaties between princes the right was limited only partially by the agreements of allied princes to preserve hereditary rights for free servitors who were transferring their allegiance. Ivan III synthesized this tradition and lent it new significance when he claimed to be the hereditary sovereign of the entire Great Russian realm. To retain legal force, local rights and relationships required his confirmation and recognition, as if he were the sole fount of all privileges. Thus, after subjugating Tver, the grand prince's government issued to the boyars of that city official charters to their lands and gave them new titles, thereby bringing them into the fold of grand princely boyars. Not infrequently, such matters were far from mere formalities, and were considered significant matters of principle.

LAND AND ARMY

As the chief of a vast state the grand prince required a large army and many resources for its maintenance. At the center of his military forces stood his personal contingent, which included all the men of the court and which was the successor of the ancient retinue. In character the new army was an expansion of the grand prince's own force to the level of a Great Russian state army in keeping with the overall growth of hereditary centralized power in Moscow. The first steps in consolidating power and mobilizing manpower increased the number of court servitors of the grand prince while diminishing the service complements of lesser princes and boyars. The ancient basis for maintaining military forces was income from landholdings. An increase of military forces required a corresponding growth in income for which sufficient land resources were necessary. Accordingly, the government of the grand prince reexamined and harshly restructured landholdings, and bent every private right to the sovereign's will.

This process of "sorting" men and lands was to assume broad dimensions under Ivan the Terrible during the period of the so-called oprichnina, an attempt to rule directly without boyar or princely approval. The practice already had taken root in Ivan III's policy toward certain regions that had been reclaimed for his direct rule. It took on particularly threatening features of rule by force, in combination with well-tried repressive measures against insubordinate regions. Entire layers of population were resettled, as in the case of Riazan by Vsevolod III "The Big Nest." There was a punitive element in the practice of resettlement in addition to the fact that beneath its terrible and angry surface it facilitated organization of new territory and military colonization. It allowed military detachments to be concentrated in particular locales or brought to the capital.

At the end of the 1460s Ivan III removed the princes of Yaroslavl from their ancestral perches. They "said good-bye forever to their hereditary lands and gave them to Grand Prince Ivan Vasilievich." In return, he provided them with districts and manors in other parts of his realm. Thus he tore them away from their lands, destroying their influence in the process. Princely authority in the lands of Yaroslavl fell to the boyar governor sent by Moscow, who in turn reregistered the villages and towns of the former landholders in the name of the sovereign, and recruited local boyars and small nobility for crown military service. Similar assignments of local servitor landholders to the service of the Muscovite state doubtless occurred in other regions, thereby forming the nuclei of military contingents in Yaroslavl, Dmitrov, Kashin and elsewhere. All served the grand prince in personal service. However, not all able-bodied men were included; forced transfer preceded the selection of local boyars and nobles for crown service. Those selected attained the status of lesser boyars at the sovereign's court.

At the time of Vasily III the practice evolved into a standardized system. As Baron Herberstein reported, "every two or three years the sovereign would collect information by regions and enroll the lesser boyars as well as the horses and servants in their possession." Based on the district census, they would "serve according to their means" in military contingents. There was seldom any exemption from this duty. Yet, by no means all hereditary princes suffered the fate of the Yaroslavl gentry.

Most remained on their estates as powerful, privileged land-owners. Throughout the sixteenth century numerous minor officials continued as of old to serve the appanage princes and similarly placed boyars and church authorities, rather than the grand prince. Not until the threat of the oprichnina and the measures taken in the last decades of his reign did Ivan the Terrible complete the process begun by his grandfather.

LAND AND POPULATION TRANSFERS

The destruction of the liberty enjoyed by Novgorod the Great was accompanied by sweeping resettlements and transfers. Having taken Novgorod under his authority, Ivan III ordered all princely and boyar manors to transfer their servitors to his government rolls. The Novgorod boyars and lesser boyars themselves petitioned to be accepted into the grand prince's service. That was not, however, the end of the matter. The political vacillations of Novgorod society presented Ivan III with the opportunity to transfer all native boyars away from their Novgorod estates and to claim them for himself. These boyars were resettled on lands granted them in the Moscow region, and thus they became part of the service nobility of that city. Apparently, many Novgorod boyars retained their boyar titles; at least the evidence of names would so indicate. Others descended to the level of secondary state servitors as lesser boyars and courtiers.

Resettlements from Novgorod were not limited to the boyars. Toward the end of the 1480s numerous burghers and merchants were transferred, to be replaced by lesser boyars and merchants from Moscow. The grand prince granted these new-comers the homes and lands of departed citizens. The displaced Novgorodians were scattered to numerous cities throughout the Muscovite realm. The scope of these reshufflings transcended mere repressive measures. In their cruel and vicious patterns can be discerned, first of all, the establishment on the ruins of free Novgorod of a Muscovite military presence in this region. Sweeping confiscations of church, monastery and boyar lands were executed partially on the excuse of real or imagined crimes by their former owners, and partially on the claim that these lands once had belonged to the grand princes and had been acquired by Novgorod during a time of weakness of the princes of the city. For whatever reason, the new acquisitions amounted to an important territorial gain for the central government. Part of the new income generated went to support servitors, and part was divided into leased lands to provide income to the crown treasury.

From another point of view these resettlements reveal the first revolutionary experiments in concentrating by design the leading components of society, commercial capital and productive resources in the Moscow region. The procedures became customary in the later stages of Moscow's ascent. The upper class of Pskov was subjected to a similar resettlement at the time of Vasily III, when the grand prince transferred the city's leadership to his seat of government. Herberstein in no way exaggerated in claiming that the grand prince dealt freely with the lives and properties of all.

In the new military order there could be no place for allied or service princes who marched at the head of their own troops as separate tactical units alongside the grand prince's armies and acted on the field of battle as they chose. Unity of organization and command, as well as the coordinated conduct of battle, required that these nominal princes be transformed into subordinate military leaders. A military structure founded on service land tenure stood in total opposition to hereditary rights. The new structure was calculated to destroy such rights by transferring to crown control all able-bodied men and the entire resources of the people in support of the prince's army. The customs and traditions of individual rights retreated all along the line before the onslaught of autocratic might and the demands of "interests of state."

CROWN RESTRICTIONS ON LANDHOLDING

In the second half of the sixteenth century the tsar's government consistently rejected voluntary private service arrangements which might result in bonds that would overshadow obligations owed to the state. Private service relationships of this kind came to be regarded legally as the equivalent of slavery. Slavery alone was recognized as the sole form of dependency on a landholder which could remove a man from a direct relationship to the state. Thus the crucial question posed to every free man was whether to be the slave of a private individual or the servant of the sovereign. The tsar's legal code limited even this choice by forbidding minor service boyars and their descendants who had not yet served the tsar from entering private service unless the proposed master was retired from the tsar's service. Legal decrees of the tsar demanded the abrogation of service pledges given by lesser boyars, and allowed for intervention against voluntary service arrangements lacking bondage contracts. As a result internal contradictions infected the concept of voluntary servitude. Clear definition and complete clarity were demanded concerning the status of such voluntary servitors and the manner in which they had entered bondage. On the other hand, to combat fictitious arrangements that would have concealed private bondage under the guise of debt obligations, persons pledged into service came to be considered slaves. A sharp line of demarcation was drawn between the full rights of a citizen in direct subordination to the state, and any type of private dependency, which was regarded as slavery.

The process of steady government penetration into the sphere of private relationships was destroying the old seignorial order. Unavoidably, it also undermined the very institution of bondage by creating conditional and temporary forms, a process that continued until the practice of imposing service obligations to the state dissolved the institution of bondage entirely.

As step by step it dismantled the barrier posed by the private landowner between the crown and the populace, the autocracy substituted its own consistent policy of land tenure based on service. All persons capable of serving in government posts were obliged to fill them. All lands organized into estates of more or less significant size were to serve as the basis of this service. By his decree of 1556 on the "service of all persons and how they shall serve in the future," Ivan the Terrible established the standards for military service by landowners: "For every fifty desiatins of good productive land, one man and one horse with full equipment, and if the campaign is to be a distant one, two horses." This standard applied to all lands of the realm, regardless of their legal status. All land must bear an obligation. The practice of this principle meant that the very dimensions and distribution of land tenure must correspond to military needs.

The stern measures used by Grand Prince Ivan III to attain these goals must have caused great consternation among the powerful landowners. Both the isolated and the large-scale confiscations and resettlements of the gentry from their ancestral homes to other localities seemingly threatened to demolish hereditary landownership as a way of life. Grand Prince Ivan III allowed many lesser princes to hold their manors but restricted their hereditary rights by forbidding their discretionary transfer of their own lands. Under Vasily III that ban became a full-fledged statute and was extended to cover the lesser boyars as well. These regulations were reaffirmed by highest authority at the beginning of Ivan the Terrible's independent reign. But by the time of the existence of the regency council that provided private counsel to the young tsar, they had lost force to a great extent. The influential circle associated with Archpriest Silvester and Alexis Adashev[1] sought to smooth the tense relations between the autocrat and his aristocratic servants. In the spirit of moribund ancient customs and traditions it permitted the return of many patrimonial estates to princely and boyar hands. The efforts of these individuals slowed the advance of tsarist autocracy. The political dichotomy then existing between the structure of crown authority and the social order as represented by governing boyar circles, so clearly depicted in the works of V.O. Kliuchevsky, merely worsened in the wake of these tactics. The final resolution of this conflict erupted in the stormy, convulsive destruction of the boyars by bloody executions. Boyar land ownership fell shattered by entire districts following the resettlements of the oprichnina period.

The legal measures of the 1360s and 1370s were directed primarily at the ancient princely manors. These estates represented dominant social and political influence and stood as the surviving symbol of the ancient independence of the hereditary princes. Yet their conversion into common hereditary estates contradicted the idea of concentrating the aggregate power of the princes of Russia in the lands of the sovereign grand prince. The appanage princes retained the broad power to dispose of their lands as they wished. The ancient aristocratic right of transfer to direct descendants also remained, although the grand prince claimed all hereditary estates where the line had died out. Under Ivan III the latter principle was formalized as a customary right of the prince of Moscow. Ivan the Terrible's legal decrees forbade to lesser princes all types of land transfer, including sale, donation to monasteries, exchange, and gifts. He stated a strict interpretation of the status of princely heirs by defining them as merely inheriting sons holding no patrimonial estates and in every instance restricted the transfer of hereditary estates by requiring the sovereign's approval. He limited the share of widows and daughters in inheritances to the amount required for their living expenses over a set period of time. Hereditary land, subjected to general service requirements, was to become part of the total pool of crown land, and determination of the extent of property rights was to stand in direct relationship to the needs and overall land policies of the state.

CHURCH LAND CLAIMS

The situation was more complex regarding church lands. The military service obligation was imposed on them as well, the forces provided by the metropolitan to form part of the grand prince's army in the same manner as those of the lesser princes. Special military leaders were appointed by the metropolitan. In Novgorod the regiment provided by the church formed a distinctive military unit under an archbishop's direct control, and all church and monastery estates provided men and equipment comparable to the boyar detachments. The importance of church lands as sources of men and equipment inevitably provoked the question of their further utilization in service of affairs of state, and this question grew pressing at the time of Ivan III. Not only the grand prince's presumptive claim to the entire lands of the realm in keeping with the hereditary nature of his authority, but also the special relationships of crown and church institutions, encouraged the grand prince's claim to direct control of church estates. A census of clerical landholding in the region of Novgorod produced the transfer of many estates to the sovereign, apparently without protest from the Russian clergy. In accomplishing this takeover, Ivan III advanced the claim that these lands belonged to the sovereign grand prince and had been acquired improperly by church institutions. Specifically, the lands had been granted by the Novgorod authorities[2] and not by charter of the grand prince, in Moscow's view the sole legitimate source of authority. This undertaking was not limited to the Novgorod region. Grand Prince Ivan III reviewed the ownership rights of monasteries over a much wider territory. Charters showing land acquisition as due to gift, purchase, or exchange were removed to the crown treasury from the St. Cyril of Belozersk monastery, for example. Lands of monasteries located near towns were appropriated for the sovereign by his officials, leaving merely a designated number of estates to the monasteries.

Concurrently Ivan III imposed several limitations on the future expansion of church land ownership. He forbade, at least in certain regions, the acquisition of hereditary property by church institutions, as well as gifts of real estate to monasteries by boyars and princes. The campaign against church estates was accompanied by enlargement of another type of church support of the state-contributions in money and in kind. Thus, when he had completed the confiscation of productive lands from the ecclesiastical institutions of Novgorod (with the blessing of Metropolitan Simon), Ivan III offered compensation by granting a charter of emolument to the Cathedral of St. Sofia from the five city quarters[3]. In studying the attempts to convert church manors into state property during the sixteenth century, A.P. Pavlov came to recognize that the measures in question concealed a comprehensive program aimed at restructuring the entire system of supporting the church. By accepting the government dole, the institutions of the church genuflected submissively and firmly to the hereditary rule of the state. But the church rose up angrily and resolutely to its own defense. In the first week of the Easter fast a proclamation appeared which declared that "all those officials who offended God's holy churches and monasteries by seizing the villages and vineyards that had been given to them, should be accursed if they did not refrain from such actions." Three hundred years later this warning was revived by the archbishop of Rostov, Arseny Matveievich, in attempting to resist the secularization of church estates by Catherine the Great[4]. The ecclesiastical leaders also offered arguments less bitter in character. In his epistles the well-known abbot of Volokolamsk monastery, Joseph,[5] invested the question of church landownership with Russian legal tradition and practice. He seemed to offer the grand prince a lesson in the history of Russian law by refuting the crown's refusal to recognize the legality of church holdings. Abbot Joseph argued that monastery and church property rights in general enjoyed dual historical and legal standing deriving from the church fathers and princely charters. The church founders in establishing cloisters had provided for these institutions through properties which, in the passage of centuries, had acquired sacred standing as donations of honorable persons to God for their eternal remembrance and the salvation of their souls. As time passed the princes had confirmed and protected these estates by imposing on violators of church rights the curse of damnation in this life and the hereafter. To support his case for immunity of those properties by stressing their sacred purposes, Joseph stated the moral claims for church property-holding. Such holdings upheld the majesty and philanthropy of the church, and guaranteed the existence of monasteries as cultural institutions and as schools for those who would become clergymen, respected and honorable persons who had taken vows.

At the Church Council of 1503, however, the question of the secularization of monastic hereditary estates was raised. It was decided that henceforth monks must live in the wilderness and subsist by their own labors. Joseph of Volokolamsk attributed this approach to this issue to Grand Prince Ivan III, who allegedly sought to take away the villages belonging to churches and monasteries. In fact this demand was advanced by a group of church idealists and ascetics led by Nil Sorsky.[6] As it turned out, simply posing the question as one to be considered in a church council as a church matter underlined the frail side of the government's position, and failed to safeguard crown interests. Grand Prince Ivan III was forced to retreat from his overly bold and direct plans for secularizing church properties. Still, his retreat should not be viewed as a notable victory for the church in countering its growing and deepening dependence on the sovereign. In practice the secular authorities retained a mechanism for mobilizing monastic and church manors in support of military needs, namely, the quartering of government officials on these lands. Joseph of Volokolamsk severely rebuked Metropolitan Serapion for giving church territories to boyars and lesser boyars. Of course, the boyars involved were secular members of the metropolitan's court. Nevertheless, these men were not exempt from state military service, and were obligated to participate in campaigns together with the forces of the hereditary and service nobility.

The general military reorganization robbed the military commanders subordinate to the metropolitan of their independent status. The contingents of troops raised by the church now joined the military forces raised by the Muscovite government. A compromise developed between the demands of the government and the claims of the ecclesiastical land holders enjoying special privileges. The agreement was reinforced by the practice of appointing church officials at the pleasure of the prince, and by the subordination of all appointments of church officials to crown authorities. The government also interfered in all other aspects of the economic and disciplinary activities in monasteries and dioceses through the Chancellory of the Royal Household and the personal decisions of the tsar. The weight of church authority continued to offer a unique safeguard against the most injurious intrusions of autocratic rule, preventing ecclesiastical landholding from being as thoroughly subjugated to the state as the boyar hereditary landlords had been.

Once prostrated to one degree or another before the demands of the crown, land ownership on a hereditary basis developed into an essential component of the Muscovite governmental edifice. It was not, however, thoroughly fused with the theoretical autocratic, patrimonial foundations of the state. The unique characteristics of land tenure as enjoyed by the princes and boyars could not survive under the new circumstances which promoted centralized ownership, and they were eliminated in the stormy times of the oprichnina. The landholding of the church preserved its established features longer by gradually adapting to the changing situation. They survived until the eighteenth century and disappeared only after experiencing bitter trials and violent reactions to evolving new relationships.

CHAPTER EIGHT

THE SERVITORS OF MUSCOVY

MILITARY SERVICE LAND TENURE

From the earliest times the evolution of patrimonial landholding had been tightly bound to the transformation of the original military retinue of the prince into territorial armies based upon true service estates. At the end of the Kievan period the military retinues, or militias, more and more began to march under the names of cities rather than princes (the Vladimir militia, the militia of Kiev, and so forth). These militia units of local landowners were grouped around the chief city of the region. Their successors were the detachments of district landowners who served the grand prince in the fifteenth century. The measures of Ivan III and his successors expanded and introduced order into these forces, and much more. The grand prince's government endeavored to participate actively in developing regional military forces and providing for their maintenance. It developed a broad local levy system and effectively linked to military purposes the land resources of Great Russia. The utilization of manorial villages and towns for supporting military servitors by means of conditional land grants long had been a method employed on monastery, ecclesiastical, boyar, and princely estates, and on lands belonging to the metropolitanate. This practice created a unique type of landholding whereby the servitors lacked the right to dispose of the estate, having no hereditary rights to it. Recruitment into the service of Moscow at the time of Ivan III was accompanied by extensive land distribution of this type. After the middle of the sixteenth century this practice solidified into a complete system of service class structuring and administration.

The decree of 1556 intended to establish a military structure that would formalize service to the tsar. Finding that many property owners held excessive amounts of land yet provided little service, the sovereign set specific regulatory standards relating service obligations to the size of an estate. He directed that landholdings be evaluated in the provinces and that excessive lands be taken from their holders and granted to persons who had none. In essence, this amounted to the same sort of redistribution that Ivan III had instituted. Now, however, stripped of its erratic and innovative character, land redistribution became an established element of regular government operations.

THE BOOK OF THOUSANDS

Administrative efforts to build an army had been launched prior to the decree of 1556 and consisted in the organization of the "Moscow thousand," which became famous in the annals of the service nobility. Tsar Ivan Vasilievich directed in 1550 that the thousand "best" military servitors be concentrated in Moscow, including lesser boyars as well as boyars and lords-in-waiting. They were to be ready at all times to perform government missions. Those holding estates close to Moscow might fulfill their Moscow service from their seats, and those who had no land in the vicinity were to receive a service estate. Service estates might be granted in addition to holders of hereditary estates when the latter were insufficient to support the servitor and his household. Thereafter the thousand positions were to be filled by the descendants of the original men. If these proved unsuitable, a selection from outside the group could be made. Service "on the Moscow list" became the dream and the crowning achievement of the careers of provincial service nobles. Deserving persons reached this distinction rarely and with great effort, as an exceptional reward and a magnanimous grant. To a significant degree the Moscow list was reserved for those with a proper genealogy.

Parallel to the establishment of the first Book of One Thousand, Moscow's crown secretaries began labors on the "State

Genealogy," which was to list the families with the greatest aristocratic standing and the closest proximity to the throne. It outlined and defined the primary genealogical attributes of those enjoying noteworthy aristocratic privileges. This social group included the thousand highest members of the aristocracy, the younger members of boyar families who were gradually advancing to the ranks of council boyars. The second level of aristocracy also rated inclusion in the state genealogy, since it contained boyars of the highest aristocratic class as well as nobles of lesser heritage who were advancing toward court and service positions ranking with the council boyars or the lords-in-waiting. The social origins of the most numerous third category in the Book of Thousands were more varied. Together with aristocratic families who had served only a short time, there were representatives of provincial gentry and even former servitors of the Novgorod boyars. Here the service record counted more than family heritage; yet a place in the Moscow list itself exalted a service family above ordinary servitors and lent its descendants priority in advancement in service and social position.

The provincial servitors yearned to reach Moscow as a means of cultivating their interests as servitors of the state and landholders. They too were divided into three categories in each district. The first and highest included persons selected from the towns to serve the usual term of three years in Moscow to supplement the leading thousand. The service of state in Moscow demanded ever increasing numbers. The men who performed this service accompanied every mission of state, acted as field commanders and chiefs of siege operations, assumed command of district military forces, foreign military formations, cossacks and musketeers[1] and the like. Service in such select capacities opened the way for direct enumeration in the Moscow list. Even so, the primary social function of such appointments lay in the selection of nobles from each district as functional cogs in the hierarchy of military command. The second provincial category included the lesser boyars of the court, who constituted the main military force in all campaigns, near or far. Numbered among this group were horsemen, infantry and other fighting men. The third category comprised the officials holding responsibilities for garrison, siege and militia activities in the towns.

THE SERVICE NOBILITY

The entire landholding class of military servitors thus was distributed in a hierarchy similar to the state organization serving the sovereign. No single rule of selection by category governed the assignments received by the members of this hierarchy. The missions given to military servitors stressed the importance of the personal character and integrity of the servitor. At the same time the entire system rested upon the need to provide for the material well-being of the landholder, who was to report for a campaign with horses, men and weapons, according to the rule of "a man and horse fully outfitted, and two horses for distant campaigns." Service at Moscow cost even more dearly, for missions and embassies were to be underwritten largely by the persons to whom they were entrusted. State salaries were quite rare. They were granted only after two years of successful service, and the salary was paid for the third year of tenure in an assignment. At times other, special arrangements were made. The tsar's disbursements were austere and were thought to be honoraria or rewards for particularly outstanding or lengthy service. In the execution of its business the crown relied upon the exploitation of both the physical and the material resources of its servants.

To be sure, the government had created these physical and material resources when it granted estates in exchange for or augmentation of a servitor's patrimonial lands. The state had established the service nobility as a class, and had added to its number by constant recruiting. In practical terms there was no

way that this group might have salvaged any political independence. Its very nature colored it as a mechanism of the
structure of state. The gamut of societal relationships at the
district level was created and shaped by the territorial system
of mobilization and by the administrative procedures practiced
in all public business. Periodically auditors from Moscow arrived
in the districts to review the activities of local officials. They
prepared lists which enumerated local officials according to
categories, in consultation with the appropriate local assessors.
The latter were selected nobles of the district who were held
accountable for the honesty of the census. These undertakings
did more than merely shape the service hierarchy into categories. They also contributed to the fixing of the military
service obligation of estates. The land grants actually assigned
to minor nobles were based on, but seldom equaled, the calculations of these census figures.

SERVICE CATEGORIES

A certain internal contradiction permeated these government
initiatives dealing with the service nobility. It centered on the
meaning attributed to the genealogical origins and aristocracy
of the noble in question. Servitors were placed in categories
according to their service records and the specifics of their
estates, with ancestry as an added criterion. The sum combination of all three differing standards determined the standing of
the servitor. Consequently, an aristocrat might lose status because of some aspect of his personal service or failure in managing his estate while a non-aristocrat might advance, even as
high as the "Moscow list," on the basis of extraordinary success. Thus talent might allow its holder to create a new and
higher aristocratic position for his descendants. While it was
said that the sovereign did not bestow ancestry, it was also
clear that without high favor the price might be poverty,
whereas new distinction might accrue to a family through the

graciousness of the tsar. Hereditary land ownership played a role throughout this system, but it gradually declined and lost its specific features as a legal institution, falling to the level of conditional possession based on service.

NEW PROVINCIAL GENTRY

It was impossible to confine the military service structure solely to nobles and lesser boyars. Unrelenting defense needs in the border lands were increasingly difficult to satisfy. In its inexorable advance to the south Moscow progressively extended the fortified frontier outward from the heartland. The advance overran the areas of free colonization and hauled new colonists in its wake. Fortifications and border defenses promoted the construction of new cities and towns in the provinces, following which the state absorbed such local military forces as the cossacks and their atamans.[2] A series of garrison formations appeared partly through transfers, partly through the free influx of adventurous soldiers from other locales, and partly by engaging vagabonds for military service. This new group of servicemen was supported by grants of small estates in the areas being defended. Frequently a whole group of servitors was allotted an area of land within common boundaries by means of a general land grant. Large numbers of soldiers manning the defense lines were drawn from migrating peasants who settled in their new homes on contract service.

A new, colorful and unique group of military servitors now emerged. Its composition continually in flux, and its life and sustenance governed by the peasant way, this social group held a position intermediate between the nobles of the lower ranks and the peasantry. These predecessors of the future small-holding service gentry[3] remained outside the military system based on the landed army. These were fighting men who served under contract agreements, in contrast to the military servitors whose social position and attitudes rested on the class principle of service according to aristocratic lineage.

Overall, the organization of military service by social groups, which was directly and tightly linked to the central authorities, forged new lines of rule radiating from the tsar's throne to replace the old ones. The boyars watched the withering of their once paramount place in politics and government. The great landowners of the type associated with the medieval feudal lord stumbled back before the new social force represented by the middle and small landowning groups composed of provincial gentry and hereditary landowners.

CHAPTER NINE

THE POPULATION OF MUSCOVY

MERCHANTS AND CRAFTSMEN

The structure of the service nobility and of land tenure concentrated both the human might of Muscovite Russia and the resources of its lands in the hands of its supreme ruler. The commercial and industrial groups also contributed to the mobilization of Muscovy's human and physical inventory of trade and capital, for the needs of state.

Following the subjugation of Novgorod the government of Ivan III extended its own procedures for collecting customs and duties to that region. Weights and measures were included in calculating tariffs, and special attention went to establishing a regional and provincial market. The authorities of Great Russia employed financial pressures to discourage the free rural district and village markets, for these exchanges allowed the peasants to avoid crown agents and tax collectors. Ivan III's decrees restricting travelling merchants to cities and official trading posts carried a ban on commercial excursions to rural districts and monasteries. Retail trade of this kind was allowed solely to local inhabitants, who were motivated by the opportunity to trade without paying taxes. The government decrees established trading posts at authorized market fairs, where the punishment for violations included confiscation of the transgressor's entire wares. New trading points originated either through official initiatives or in response to popular petitions. At times a market might be moved from place to place. Trade might begin at a new location on condition that it be sufficiently distant from neighboring and established markets to avoid serious competition that might create tax losses.

Such strict regulation of domestic commerce led to forced transfers of merchants and craftsmen from one town to another in keeping with the spirit of Muscovite organizational methods. In crushing once powerful Novgorod, Ivan III forcibly resettled boyars, citizens and numerous merchants alike. It is quite obvious that his political measures were of national economic significance. Ivan III's commercial policy toward Novgorod was intended more to guide foreign trade development than to affect domestic commercial procedures. In alliance with Denmark, he initiated the century-long struggle for free trade on the Baltic Sea. In contesting Swedish dominance simultaneously he suppressed the Hanseatic[1] trade of Novgorod in order to transfer Western trade relations to Moscow.

From this moment the concentration of important traders, warehouses, and foreign commerce in Moscow played a vital role in the growth of the Great Russian state. Coercive government measures forced merchants to move from the provinces to Moscow. From there they were resettled by official decree to various towns as directed by the government's trade calculations. Manufacturers and craftsmen needed by the sovereign's court and the capital were transferred from the places where they had won renown and proficiency. During the second half of the sixteenth century there emerged a comprehensive system for organizing the merchant and industrial groups comparable to the service nobility structure. This class was subordinated no less completely to the will of the sovereign in its entire activities and professional endeavors. Its leaders were drawn from the mightiest merchant capitalists, foreign representatives, and domestic and foreign directors of wholesale commerce. Their operations assumed an official cast and the sovereign came to grant merchants honorary titles so exalted that an insult to one of the "honored merchants"[2] was regarded, in the tsar's law code, as ten times greater than an insult to an ordinary citizen. These honored merchants were exempted from normal taxation and obligations, for they were regarded not as ordinary subjects but as distinguished notables. They owned manors on a par with the service nobility, and legally were subject solely to the central law court of the grand prince. Ordinarily such a court was convened by the boyar who controlled the state treasury.

The honored merchants also staffed the chief financial offices of the tsar and grand prince. They were responsible for tax collecting and also supervised the sale of government goods. Along with sworn officials from lower levels of the Moscow merchantry and provincial merchants, they were in charge of managing customs and stocking crown warehouses "on their honor," and they directed the crown salt and fishery monopolies. The honored merchants together with the sworn officials were obliged to make a set annual payment based on their prices, as determined by prior payments or new assessments. They were expected to make good shortages from their own purses; were they unable to do so, the merchant corporations could be charged to make payment. The service of honored merchants in close proximity to the crown was more singular in character. It might be performed through other merchant or manufacturing groups either by selection or by rotation as established by the corporations as a whole. In addition to collecting various taxes and state incomes, the honored merchants and other merchants were required to appraise crown-owned commodities such as sable and other furs received as tribute from the tribes and peoples of the northeastern borders, and later from Siberia. The profitable sale of these pelts also was entrusted to the honored merchants.

The deputies of crown officials and sworn officers with various financial responsibilities at times included merchants from the ranks of traders and cloth merchants who were gathered in Moscow as corporations of distinguished merchants. These were augmented as necessary by wealthy merchants of Moscow and provincial town guilds, which complained and wailed that the government was emasculating their commercial and financial strength by systematically removing their strongest and most established members. To maintain control of this guild-like merchantry, the government formed taxation groups known as local hundreds.[3]

The remaining citizens also were grouped according to their wealth, and given regular duties both at home and on missions to nearby towns. They fulfilled their government obligation according to communal practice, approaching in their way of life and customs the peasants inhabiting the districts belonging to the crown, particularly if their service was performed in small settlements. In the North, this similarity between the townsman and the peasant of the rural district grew especially pronounced. Their economic activities whether as farmers or artisans were comparable, and together they comprised a uniform social layer inhabiting the districts. When the Time of Troubles[4] summoned them to political action, they stepped forward as a unified social force.

THE TAXPAYING POPULATION

The town dwellers and crown peasants made up the taxpaying population of the Muscovite state. The division between tax obligations and military service responsibilities came about only gradually. Vestiges of the general military obligation were still to be observed in the sixteenth century and even at the dawn of the seventeenth century when, because of unusual emergencies, merchants had to be pressed into garri on service. On the other hand, a transition gradually eroded the tax privileges of hereditary landowners in favor of the general exemption from personal financial obligation due members of boyar households. The taxpaying obligations of peasants on gentry and patrimonial estates were preserved. In the eyes of the crown, the population was divided into two basic spheres according to whether one paid in the form of service or taxes, whether one served the crown as officials or peasants.

During the fourteenth and early fifteenth centuries the term "dependents" was applied to persons living on princely or monastery lands. A distinction was drawn between this group and the free peasants inhabiting the same estates because the former were constrained by some degree of bondage. Distinctions of this kind are found in the official documents of the period and in other, rarer documents dealing with secular and private land ownership. These poor folk, forerunners of impoverished Russians who lived under strict supervision on princely or ecclesiastical estates, did not enjoy the right of resettlement. It is they rather than the "old dwellers"[5] who were the ancestors of the later bonded serfs. Whereas the charters when mentioning movements of peasants from one landowner to another used the terms "he left" and "he was accepted," regarding the poor they stated that "he escaped" and that the new landowner "recaptured" him. As the hereditary state developed, the term "poor" came to denote the entire taxed populace as viewed by the government of the grand prince. This corresponded to the designation of the former free servitors as state servitors. Both terms carried the connotation of limited civil rights, and served to signify the new order of subordination of the individual to the supreme authority of the sovereign tsar and grand prince. The hereditary nature of state rule found clear expression in this new terminology, as it did in the general concept that all lands within the borders of the realm belonged directly to the sovereign grand prince. It should be noted in this connection that the free departure of peasants from their lands affected plowing, planting, and harvesting, including farming on the common lands belonging to the grand prince. Thus sales agreements read "I will sell you crops and labor from the lands of the grand prince, but the meadows and pasture lands are ours." This understanding of the system of tax obligations to the crown lay at the core of the peasants' position in the Muscovite state.

RURAL DISTRICT ADMINISTRATION

The total hereditary authority of the grand prince over the rural peasant populace required instruments of enforcement. Therefore, crown agents were appointed to live among the people, much like the village bailiffs of crown and patrimonial manors. This power apparently was to be wielded by rural district officials appointed to each country district by the grand prince. The crown governor retained authority only over the high criminal court in matters of murder and litigation crossing district lines. The appointed rural district chief sat at the head of the rural district council and with granted authorization participated in its deliberations. His conversations with the village elder and the peasants enabled him to distribute the district's common lands, unoccupied farmsteads, and so forth. He was empowered to initiate legal proceedings jointly with the district peasant commune and its representatives.

The lack of records makes it difficult to determine the degree to which the rural district administration blanketed the country during the time of Ivan III. Certainly, however, it did not play the role intended for it. It did not become the base from which to develop a comprehensive crown administration of the hereditary lands or the human resources of the nation. Then, in the middle of the sixteenth century, an abrupt change occurred in the administrative structure of the Muscovite state. The appointed officials who received maintenance from the local population and the rural district chiefs were replaced by the civil and land institution known as the "land."

The hereditary character of crown administration affected the every-day social and legal life of the peasantry much more than it did administrative practice. The government regarded the peasants strictly from the point of view of tax procedures and privileges accorded to landowners. The policy expressed in the grant charters earlier issued by the crown foreshadowed the autocratic, hereditary order that took roots in the land

tenure sphere of peasant rural districts. These charters had introduced the principle that the decisions of the grand prince
overruled the precedents established by popular common law.
The division of unimproved rural areas into inheritable lands,
and grants of entire rural districts to aristocratic newcomers in
return for their service to the crown, were but pale harbingers
of the coming destruction of the rural customs and rights associated with the system of territorial militias based on estate grants.
As the service nobility began to acquire land, the peasant rural
districts dissolved into manors and the fragmented districts disappeared. The rural district structure and the functions of its
council fell to the service landowner, who was authorized to
impose financial and work obligations on the peasants for his
personal benefit, while also collecting taxes from them for the
crown. His authority stood between the peasants and the crown,
to whom he answered for all government interests in the villages
of his manor. Official documents indicate that it was he rather
than the peasants who was responsible for payment of the
crown taxes. If necessary, he might receive tax exemptions as
well. Because of his responsibility for maintaining order in his
villages, the landowner acquired administrative and legal authority over the populace. Furthermore, he inherited the activities
of the rural district council in economic matters, and therefore
determined the disposition of unoccupied lands and the policy
of attracting new settlers. In exercising his economic responsibilities he was to obey the crown's injunction not to lay waste
to his estate. Failure to prevent such abuse would result in confiscation of the estate by the sovereign.

In the regions where land ownership by the service nobility
as manors and hereditary lands was concentrated, the southern
and western fringes of Muscovy, the peasant rural communes
were utterly dismembered and destroyed by the new land own-
nership system in the course of the sixteenth century. It was
in these areas, where Muscovy's military forces were gathered
along defensible border lines, that new aggregations of servitors

were found. After the Time of Troubles the need for restoring military power became particularly acute. Part of the western border was in foreign hands, while other sectors lay thoroughly desolated and threatened by new dangers. Consequently, land grants were made in the northeastern districts of the region to the northeast of Moscow. Thereupon the rural districts made up of crown peasants disappeared almost completely in the central part of Muscovy and survived only in the distant northern coastal region.

LAND AND LABOR

The land designated for estate grants to the service nobility was by no means rich or highly productive. Customarily the estates proved to be smaller than anticipated, a circumstance that forced their holders to search out ways to compensate for the divergence between the expectation and the actual land received. It was not merely the rural districts and the hereditary lands taken by the sovereign which were distributed. Crown lands as well often were used, albeit with great caution and restraint. Although the crown lands were abundant, the kind of inhabited lands necessary to support the servitors proved to be scarce. Truly, therefore, the harnessing of the human and natural resources of Muscovy in service to the crown was hampered greatly by the sparse population density of Muscovite Russia. Not surprisingly, the government stood under constant pressure to hold labor and taxpayers on the land and to husband these resources. Ever since the days when tribute was paid to the Tatar khan, efforts were made to protect the chief source of wealth, the taxed peasantry and their lands. This resource would not be squandered on the prince's household, or used to grant hereditary lands to boyars or monasteries. This policy was reinforced by the desire of the taxpaying communes to maintain their identity as labor and payment units. They wanted to hold their members, except for those who liquidated their holdings and their relationship to the rural commune by transferring both to a new member who would take their place. There was no other lawful way to leave the district commune; those who left without finding a replacement could be forced to return as violators of their civil obligations. Naturally, this conditional tie to the land for tax purposes, and through it to the rural district and the household, under the pressure of severe labor shortages evolved into the unconditional bondage of the peasants (and their city counterparts). This process and its institutionalization in society culminated during the seventeenth century.

RESETTLEMENT OF PEASANTS

The systematization of crown tax procedures fixed the obligations of the inhabitants of titled hereditary lands as well as of the service manors. However, where noble land ownership and administration prevailed, local authority passed to the landowner, even if he retained the village commune mechanism to administer the estate. The landowner naturally wished to keep the old settlers of his estate, inasmuch as his ability to satisfy his own service obligations depended directly on his income. Moreover, he was responsible for preventing the decline of his estate. The only real source of new people to live in the village was the free, unobliged and untaxed rural populace. The persons most interested in settling on virgin lands were the younger, landless members of peasant families and villagers who did not have enough land. The sons of fathers, the brothers of brothers, the nephews of uncles, and all whose presence burdened their neighbors, were invited to settle virgin lands. It was only the taxpaying old settlers who dared not yield to the blandishments of the newly-arrived landowners. The old settlers might move onto virgin lands only when in so doing they would not harm the rural district; namely, by finding a replacement.

The newly-arrived landowner and the new relationships he introduced meant added complications for the taxed rural population. The settlement of virgin lands forced the newly-arrived peasants into some degree of dependency on the land-owner, economically as well as legally and administratively. The actual economic status of manorial peasants has been incorrectly assessed in Russian scholarly literature by seeking to view it as a version of tenant farming. To live on someone's land as a peasant did not mean being a tenant. The attraction of peasants to newly-acquired estates was a method that involved more than simply the collection of rent for the sake of income, whether in money or in kind, based on harvest sharecropping. The addition of peasants built up the labor force of the estate and expanded its cultivated lands. This method aided the landowner in structuring the economic activities of a hereditary or newly-granted estate.

Thus the landowner would provide to the peasant land, a hut and other farm buildings and equipment, along with seed grain and food until the first harvest. This investment was returned by the transformation of the land plot from virgin soil into tilled land. Sometimes the peasant would go into debt at the extremely high rates of interest customary in primitive economic conditions. Now the landlord had a labor force that could be exploited for rents, additional collections, and labor in his household and activities. There is no basis for equating these relationships with the simple institution of tenant rent. The dimensions and composition of the obligations were determined by local customs and traditions, which in the case of large, well-managed monastery estates might be formulated as a set of regulations with the force of law. But in the everyday life of hereditary estates, things went along according to the practical customs and conditions of farming. With no other sanction than the possible loss of his estate through its ruination, the landowner established rules that were sufficiently clear and stable to be included as part of income and collection procedures in official charters. For the first several years newcomers usually received tax exemptions and release from other monetary obligations as incentives. Thereafter, their treatment was the same as that of the old settlers, their payments being determined by the estate's viability. In time the new settlers became accepted elements of the microcosm of the landowner's estate, itself a unique economic and administrative entity.

SERFDOM

Several limitations gradually appeared that altered this relationship. The agricultural cycle made it common-law practice to permit departures from the estate and release by the landowner only at the end of the growing season, on St. George's Day in autumn. This was codified in the Law Code of 1550, and interpreted as including the two-week period preceding and following November 26. Landowners insisted that departures be tied legally to specified times and to a complete reckoning of accounts as well. The Law Code specified the payment of one quarter of the value of the peasant farmstead for each year of residence, and the complete payment of its full value after four years. Hauling on the roads in winter was prescribed, but the Law Code annulled other fees that apparently had arisen in practice.

The reckoning of accounts was more complex if the peasant had accepted some form of legal servitude for his debt. At first an obligation so assumed held no actual connection to serfdom, and the departing peasant might take along his debt to pay later. But then lack of effective collection methods compelled the landowners to insist on payment prior to departure. Such demands were recognized as legitimate by the government. By the end of the fifteenth century the general principle was established that a peasant could not be released until his debt had been settled. Any peasant withdrawing outside the established time period or without proper notice and a financial settlement was regarded as a fugitive. He could be returned by force to his old home.

These complex demands and conditions surrounding resettlement by a peasant were the factors involved in the demise of
the personal freedom of the taxpaying peasant. Furthermore,
Russian agriculture deteriorated greatly during the second half
of the sixteenth century, and the ensuing crisis grew in direct
relation to the expansion of colonization to the south and east.
As a result, the battle of the landowners for laborers took on
extreme forms; competing nobles simply bought peasants away
from other noblemen by paying all debts that might block a
peasant from leaving an estate. Even so, change of masters
merely increased a peasant's dependence. Personal arrangements
among landowners made from time to time to end their conflicts became very much like sales of landless thralls.

Laments about massive flights from estates grew louder, and
serious disorder in the system of crown service and taxation
seemed inevitable. Concerned with the many complaints about
fugitive peasants, the artifical transfer of manpower during the
growing season and without notice, and similar problems, the
government moved to limit the complaints by establishing a
five-year statute of limitation on searches aimed at returning a
fugitive. This measure, however, which was put into practice
by the crown officials and boyars, provoked stubborn dissatisfaction among most of the service nobility. The nobility worked
diligently to have this statute set aside. At first the crown re-
lented by extending the time of grace, but even as late as the
Law Code of Tsar Alexis Mikhailovich, it had not rescinded the
law. That law code offered a further and even more important
boon to the nobility by institutionalizing the permanent serfdom of all peasants of a manor. Heretofore only the heads of
households, as recorded in the census, had been bound to their
lands to such a degree.

These concessions to the demands of the landowning nobility not only coincided with the interests of the state, they
also introduced improvements into the system of maintaining military manpower. Numerous petitions from the service

nobility indicated that a true accounting of the resources necessary for supporting their military service obligations required calculation of the labor force in terms of the number of manorial peasant households. After the destruction of the boyar class the crown found its chief pillar in the landowning nobility. Consequently, it was forced to place the nobility's interests ahead of the rights of the laboring village populace. Near the end of the sixteenth century, accordingly, the government issued several decrees designed to halt peasant migrations and relocations into certain areas, or to particularly large landholdings. Peasant resettlement was limited to designated years and to set periods, as decreed by the sovereign. Boris Godunov[6] granted such a period of permitted departures over a time span of two years to selected landowners, as forced resettlements. After the Time of Troubles resettlement in all its forms disappeared from the Russian scene, continuing to exist solely in the dreams of peasants, in recollections of the periodic years of resettlement, and in reproaches to the tsar that "former tsars had permitted departures, but the present sovereign allows none."

The tsardom of Muscovy had prepared thoroughly for the levelling of peasants and slaves which was completed by Peter the Great's tax reform legislation. The peasants on patrimonial lands and the estates of the service nobility now became serfs, belonging to their masters on the basis of documents of various types, ranging from revenue and population census records, to deeds of sale and wills. They were not attached to the land, but directly to the landowner. In his law code Tsar Alexis viewed the serfs in this way, as living property of the landlord, when he recognized their negotiable value to the master. They became legal collateral for their master's debts, and could be delivered from one landlord to another in compensation for fugitive peasants, in the same value, from the indebted landowner's manor.

During the period of the Russian empire the rural district peasants and the crown peasants, divested of their rights by the

Muscovite state, came to be regarded as state serfs. Besides their normal taxes and labor obligations, a special rent was exacted from them, similar to that paid by serfs to their noble masters. Later, during the nineteenth century, these state serfs fell under the jurisdiction of the Ministry of State Domains. The roots of the autocracy of Muscovy lay set in the utter enslavement of all classes of the people.

CHAPTER TEN

THE GOVERNMENT OF MUSCOVY

The political edifice of the tsardom of Muscovy was built on the autocratic rule of all human and material resources of the country. The exertion of power required unceasing and very intensive efforts by the central authorities in the areas of organization and administration.

The group most suitable for administering the hereditary autocracy was the corps of crown officials. However, the rural district chiefs of Muscovite Russia did not become the nucleus of the emerging Moscow bureaucracy. The vast territory, the dispersed populace, and poor domestic communications made the task of creating a durable administrative network based on existing institutions too much for the Muscovite state. The rural district leaders continued to be locally-supported crown officials, just as were the appointed governors before them. They represented the boyar administrative system, and burdened the central government with heavy expenses and frequent demands, oppressing the populace and providing little in return. The rural district leaders contributed neither to the affairs of state nor to the elementary needs of preserving order and security in local life. The elimination of these antiquated offices became the task confronting the Muscovite state as it plunged into the sixteenth century.

LOCAL ADMINISTRATION REFORMS

By the second quarter of the sixteenth century the Muscovite regime had instituted strict reform measures in local administration. It complied with the requests and complaints of its subjects in the provinces regarding the rapid proliferation of robberies and violence, the neglect of the authorities, the few benefits and great expenses incurred by the special investigators and inspectors sent from Moscow, and so forth. The central government determined to entrust local administration to local social groups on the basis of self-government.

During the 1530s the authorities preserved the rural district communes and the town communal groups while simultaneously shifting the onerous tasks of maintaining law and order, providing police protection, and holding criminal courts, to district communal authorities representing all groups.[1] In the 1550s maintenance by the local population was withdrawn from the crown governors and rural district officials. Their duties were transferred to elected representatives of the taxed communal groups. Thereby the nascent state administration utilized ancient self-government practices in a novel way to assure tax collection, law and order, and criminal justice. The new communal elders, now armed with legal powers, were responsible for prosecuting troublemakers at all legal stages, from investigation and legal prosecution to judgement and actual execution of sentences. They were subordinate and responsible to the Chancellory for Criminal Affairs in Moscow. The village elders, town magistrates and rural judges supervised the labor and tax interests of the crown and saw to the performance of other civil obligations by the provincial inhabitants. They held courts of law for civil matters in their territory.

The crown government intended this rural reform to benefit the population, which was now relieved of the costs of maintaining the former appointed officials. Accordingly, the crown felt justified in imposing a new tax commensurate with its graciousness, namely, an annual fee to support its appointed officials. In reality, therefore, the newly-instituted local administration was more an added burden than a new privilege. The principle of joint responsibility and mandatory contributions of money and "voluntary" labor to the state lay at the basis of the communal institutions of the sixteenth century. It was similar in theory to the financial procedures used to extract services from the merchant guild of Moscow and the provincial merchantry.

CENTRALIZATION

The large-scale "voluntary" service imposed throughout all branches of government made it possible for the state to function with a highly simplified administrative system adapted to exploit in its own interests the entire human and economic capacity of the country. Yet this system was not well-suited to the more complex and creative undertakings of a centralized government. In the existing circumstances the crown required permanent representatives only in certain locations for specific purposes. There were military commanders at border cities, city magistrates at fortified towns, and so forth. All other administrative affairs might be supervised by public groups and their elected representatives, or by temporary missions sent from Moscow to execute urgent assignments. The relatively primitive national economy and the poorly developed domestic cultural and economic communications between individual regions of Great Russia narrowed the tasks and diminished the pressure of directing public life. The central authorities in Moscow wished to institute only those forms of administration that would guarantee the punctual delivery of services and taxes with the least expenditure of manpower and resources. By subjecting to its authority the entire gamut of the most important land ownership, commerce, and manufacturing interests, Moscow created within each interest group the tools necessary to control that group. These were the groups holding pivotal significance in managing the basic economic enterprise of the country. The remaining concerns of government might safely be left to the local public organizations charged with carrying on self-government. The result was the extremely centralized public and political structure of the Muscovite state, dictated by the necessity of advancing crown interests. Above this hierarchy were situated the boyar council and the administrative chancellories, the directing institutions of the central government.

DECLINE OF THE BOYAR COUNCIL

There is disagreement among Russian scholars (Sergeevich in opposition to Kliuchevsky[2]) revolving around the question as to whether the boyar council was an institution in the strict sense this term acquired in the legally-formulated bureaucratic administrative structure. The extent of the dispute is expressed in Sergeevich's paradoxical assertion that the directive in the Muscovite law code concerning the normal procedure for issuing new statutes requiring approval by all the boyars was an attempt to limit the tsar's autocratic power. Rather, the absolutist government sought to convert the boyar council into a high crown office whose personnel and activities would be determined by the authorities. Because it preserved the traditional aristocratic nature of the boyar council, and the independent political influence of the boyars, the boyar council fit poorly into the framework of crown administration. It was required to carry out executive and advisory functions at a high level. The demise of boyar tradition and power during the cruel years of Ivan the Terrible's reign prepared the way for .the transformation of the boyar council into an institution with no policy role whatsoever. It became the colorless political and social tool of the tsar. The "assembly of all the boyars" lost all real importance in the seventeenth century, and became nothing more than a ceremony of pomp and circumstance in support of the tsar's government. The actual business of state was accomplished either in meetings of boyars close to the sovereign, or through individual boyar commissions and administrative sessions of the "Chamber of Settlement."[3] Such transformation of the boyar council became possible and inevitable as a result of the final triumph of the bureaucracy throughout the Muscovite administrative system.

MUSCOVY IN CRISIS

The domination and rapid development of the bureaucratic structure in Muscovite government life was the primary political result of the great crisis experienced at the beginning of the seventeenth century. The conditions that brought about this trial were rooted deeply in the structure of Muscovite Russia's national life and institutions. Confined by the pressures of the Tatars and Lithuania, Great Russia under the rule of Moscow created a strong and lasting domestic order. An autocratic government, itself struggling for survival, had gathered and tempered the might of Great Russia and forged a national state. With the inevitability of destiny and formed by given geographic features, Great Russia grew from a defensive society into an aggressive power which crushed the barriers holding back a new surge of colonization to the south and east.

The struggle for commercial and colonization routes brought Great Russia a series of quick successes far beyond its ethnic limits. The conquest of the Trans-Volga region and entry into the Don river basin, together with the approach through Novgorod to the Baltic Sea, left the historically young state with immense political problems in ruling the complex, vast and unstable East European plain. Russia's newly gathered and loosely organized forces were stretched thin, and the cost was a serious unravelling of the economic, social and governmental fabric of its central regions. The colonization of the new lands and their promise of agricultural and industrial raw materials, in addition to the established attractions of the old migratory and commercial routes, stirred the people of Great Russia and lured them to a new venture.

The second half of the sixteenth century witnessed the expanding international influence of Muscovy. But at that very moment the foundations of national economic life were experiencing a growing crisis. The social and political structure of the Muscovite state was shaken by the Time of Troubles, and a severe economic conflict was provoked by the disharmony between the apparently strong and organized country and the unanswered demands of the times. The literature of the period of Ivan the Terrible overflowed with troubled, grim presentiments. A trembling was felt beneath the edifice of the Great Russian state as it convulsed and dissipated its strength in the fluid vastness of Eastern Europe. The feverish administrative measures of Ivan Vasilievich (the Terrible), the oprichnina repressions and the village council reforms "chopped the land in two as if with an axe." Tsar Ivan's overwrought character and actions reflected the elemental forces released by the conflict between autocratic Muscovy's international position and the widening schism in its domestic life.

The economic crisis pushed the conflicting interests at work in society to their extremes. During the Time of Troubles a heated struggle had erupted between various social groups. The ripening crisis produced the great collapse of the Muscovite state at the very moment that the fall of the dynasty cracked the outer shell of tradition. The result was a fearful catastrophe for a state built on the foundation of a hereditary monarchy. The lack of succession tested the capability of Muscovy to maintain unity without the strong central ruler who had created it. The tsarist government had won strength and had become a thorough autocracy, destroying in the process the independent administrative influence of both the church and the boyars. It had created other administrative tools—the highly-centralized service nobility and the taxpaying groups. The entire burden of executing the affairs of state fell on the military service landowners, merchants and artisans. The clergy, boyars, and councillors of the tsar had been reduced to the position of a crown council attached to the sovereign and without independent political influence.

THE ASSEMBLY OF THE LAND

As the Livonian War expanded into a more dangerous conflict with the Polish-Lithuanian Commonwealth, Ivan the Terrible turned elsewhere in gauging the national strength and for support in the difficult decision whether to continue the struggle for free access to the Baltic and for the West Russian lands. For "counsel with all the ranks of the Muscovite state" he turned to the Assembly of the Land.[4] This unique type of governmental deliberative body was the natural product of the sharp social reorientation that had taken place in Muscovy. The former councils, composed of the boyars, and the officials of the boyar council and local administration, together with the holy synod of the clergy and at times an even broader body called together from the state service nobility, had been unable to provide sufficient information as to the actual state of affairs in the country. This was even more true after the abolition of the practice of supporting crown officials at local expense. These earlier consultative bodies had failed to express the opinion of the nation as a whole, which was essential if the activities of the tsar's government were to be based on actual circumstances. Similarly, the district communes of the sixteenth century were, in the expression of V.O. Kliuchevsky, nothing more than consultations of the government with its own agents. The structure of the national administration was quite different, and consequently, the composition of the Assembly had to change. Chancellery officials, the various servitors, and groups from the commercial and artisan organizations were summoned.

The convention of all classes of the Muscovite state together with the boyar council and the holy synod formed the body that came to be known as the Assembly of the Land. At the twilight of the sixteenth century, when the old dynasty of Muscovy's sovereigns came to an end, an Assembly of this nature was called upon to act as the primary national political force. It selected Boris Godunov to mount the vacant throne. During the troubled years of collapse when an intense search was made for a way to restore legitimate government authority, it was realized that the needed strength could be generated only through the deliberations of all Russian subjects. Organized social groups, such as the boyars and clergy, the service nobility, and the taxpaying people who were united through representatives in the district communes, comprised the focus of political power in the Assembly that formed the provisional government of boyars led by Dmitry Pozharsky[5] and his compatriots. Next, the Assembly selected Michael Romanov[6] to father the new dynasty of imperial Russia.

The Assembly of the Land had a composition different than its sixteenth-century predecessors. The formal distinctions seemed slight to contemporaries. The methods for selection for various duties and functions were defined so broadly that appointment to participate in the Assembly seemed little different than a government appointment to attend one of the assemblies of the sixteenth century. Representatives were chosen by the same procedures in the seventeenth century that had been used earlier to select officials of police and district institutions. These appointees took their places alongside the Moscow service nobility, which served on such deliberative bodies without special appointments. But the basic purpose of these delegates was to voice at the Assembly the desires and demands of the social element they represented. They worked conscientiously to breathe life into this charge, with the result that they constituted a new and important aspect of the Muscovite scene as popular, or perhaps more accurately, class advocates.

The Assemblies of the Land in Muscovite Russia often have been compared to Western European assemblies which included representation from all estates or classes. Indeed, in general structure and in the role they were called to play at this crucial juncture in the country's political life, there is a great deal of similarity. The deep and significant difference rests in the level of development attained by such assemblies in various Western European countries, in contrast to their fate in Russia. In its own unique manner and in contrasting circumstances, Muscovite Russia was experiencing that moment in a country's historical life usually termed in Western Europe a "class monarchy." The basic difference may be understood if it is realized that in Western European countries the appearance of classes was an essential and crucial factor in the very emergence of central governments from the ruins of feudalism. In Russia, the assemblies of the land facilitated the transferral of the conduct of national affairs to an autocratic monarchy. The gathering of power into the hands of the central government was completed when the dwarf principalities of the petty hereditary aristocracy succumbed to Muscovy. The authorities in Moscow summoned the recognized groups in society to participate in deliberations and decisions concerning governmental matters. Society did not, as in the West, hold any measure of actual political power. Instead, society rendered service and fulfilled its obligation to do the sovereign's bidding. On the other hand, the very fact that, at a crucial time, the crown sought the advice of all ranks of the Moscow citizenry reflected an attempt to find the succor and support of Russian society. In so doing the government failed to uphold the standards of absolute obedience it had interposed between itself and its servants and charges.

The leading social groups had been summoned to participate in meaningful ways in government during the sixteenth century. Now the crisis in ruling the country, a key political feature of the Time of Troubles, again forced the authorities to resort to substantial elective and delegative undertakings. The cause of the moral and social sin of "senseless silence throughout the world," in the opinion of a contemporary philosopher, was the wrath of God which took the form of a massive collapse. Russia might be redeemed were the Assembly to labor mightily to save the motherland and the shattered state order, and if the welfare of the state as well as private interests would guide social and political relations. The welfare of the state must be understood in the broad sense as reflecting unique local needs and desires, as distinct from the narrow purposes and interests of the hereditary state authority.

In experiencing the great Moscow tragedy, as the Poles called the Time of Troubles, Muscovite society awakened to act on its own. Muscovite society had been molded by the old regime and disciplined to provide service and taxes. Pressed by coercion into rural district and town compartments where it stored energy thanks to the centralized system for managing the service landowners, merchants and artisans, Russian society now burst the constricting bonds of narrow local interests. The Time of Troubles made clearer than ever the value of national unity in land and commercial matters. It was the local leaders who set about restoring order in Muscovy after the Time of Troubles.

THE SEARCH FOR STABILITY

Nevertheless, great burdens remained on the shoulders of the servitors and the taxpaying population because of the heavy hand of the tsar and grand prince wielded during the reign of Ivan the Terrible. It was not merely the boyars who suffered from his highhandedness. The wanton excesses of sovereign anger merely descended more brightly and painfully on them, for they were affected directly by the degrading eccentricities of the tsar's suspicions and the cruel convulsions of his turbulent soul. They sought protection from his caprice by demanding guarantees of personal and property rights, which they might have obtained had they followed legal procedures in the deliberations of the boyar council. They protested the neglect of established administrative practices in preparing crown statutes after decisions had been reached in boyar deliberative meetings. The fundamental principles of traditional jurisprudence in question actually went far beyond simple rectification of banishments and idiosyncracies of individual legal rulings. In an ultimate sense they underscored the lack of civil rights enjoyed by crown servitors and peasants in dealing with autocratic, hereditary government and its officials. In the sworn statement given by Tsar Vasily Shuisky the boyars insisted on the welfare of all subjects in addition to their own yearning for remedies against arbitrary rule. Tsar Vasily swore on the cross[7] to all Orthodox Christians that he would judge them by just and righteous procedures and never deliver them unto their enemies unjustly, and that he would protect them from all oppression.

The fluctuations of public opinion in the stormy years of the Time of Troubles amplified this protest against the precariousness of all personal and property rights under the prevailing hereditary order of government and administration. When the middle levels of the service and taxed population arose to defend Muscovy against foreign intruders and domestic malcontents, they were also seeking to restore institutions to safeguard the people against official abuses visited on them by the state, and the oppression of the mighty. They wished to ensure legality in the proceedings of the courts and in the administration of crown and public affairs. The favorable circumstances of the moment permitted this quest to produce a direct statement of the basic political question revolving around the practice of unrestricted and self-serving supreme government. The agreement to elect Prince Wladyslaw[8] to the tsarist throne established a limitation on absolute power by requiring that the tsar consult with the boyar council, the boyar law court and the "Council of all the Land."[9] The effectiveness of the temporary government in the Moscow mobilization of 1611, as well as in the second Nizhni Novgorod mobilization,[10] underlined the importance of the approval of the rural districts as the primary source of all executive and legal authority.

This outcome of the political problem was made possible by the exceptional circumstance in which a people found itself without a government, and by the attempt to install a foreign candidate of another faith on the Russian throne.[11] The Assembly had to act quickly to grant to the military commanders the authority they needed to conduct the business of state. This action did not represent some new political doctrine founded on the notion of popular rule. It was spawned by concerns for Russia's vital interests in a situation of political crisis. The underlying tendencies in Russian society, which was in all respects extremely conservative, were quite different. What was wanted was the restoration of the traditional political order, under a dynasty of native sovereigns. Much effort has been squandered by historians in seeking positive meaning in the well-known formal restrictions on the power of newly-elected Tsar Michael. That entire question remains debatable to the present day but the confusion is understandable because, in addition to the factor of the supposed limits placed on the tsar's power at the dawn of the seventeenth century, there were present in society other, more weighty and historically more significant factors. The period in question, after all, had witnessed devastating blows to the entire fabric of public life.

THE ALLIANCE OF CROWN, LANDOWNERS AND MERCHANTS

The urge for lasting peace throughout the country and reestablishment of public order fostered new and more reasonable outlooks on government administration which involved the popular will and the Almighty as well as the sovereign. Life itself posed with increasing insistence the need to bring order to the country. The bold exploitation of people and resources for the needs of state was no longer acceptable. Yet the evolution of the very concept of the responsibility of government, characteristic of the seventeenth century, led in the final analysis to the replacement of the hereditary monarchy by a police state, with its system of "enlightened" guardianship of all facets of national life in the name of the general "well-being." This new orientation evolved gradually out of the extremely severe conditions experienced in Muscovite government and public life. The service landowners and taxed town merchants managed to codify the given social configuration and thereby to safeguard the rights they had acquired. They were not motivated by hopes of participation in the supreme councils of government; rather, they wished to institutionalize the social order that had emerged as a legal, class-oriented system. Their aspirations were directed primarily toward defending their welfare against the conflicting interests of the upper classes, the major landowners, and the lower peasant masses. This middle group held the upper hand thanks to its social influence and to the arbitrary decisions of the crown authorities. It was in a position to demand the recognition and guarantee of its class position.

In later years this middle group displayed no great political firmness. As the tested bastion of Muscovite autocracy which had matured and found form jointly with it, the middle element of society controlled the nation's basic capital resources. Its interests essentially coincided with those of the state, which during the course of the seventeenth century continued to promote noble land ownership and the advancement of commercial and manufacturing endeavors. The general welfare was regarded in terms of economic growth. Even so, this social group was weak politically because the general order of Russian socio-economic life was weak. The insignificant development of city life and commercial trade provided no underpinnings for the growing demands of the merchants and manufacturers who in Russia did not mature as a mighty economic and cultural force. Rather, social primacy in Russia fell to the landowning nobility, which preserved the social and psychological features of a service class. The legal demands of the nobility were directed at achieving the complete enserfment of the peasants by removing the statute of limitations on apprehending fugitive serfs, and eliminating the right of withdrawal for the entire manorial population rather than merely for old settler heads of households. The landowners sought an equalized distribution of state service obligations corresponding to the size of an estate's labor force, and advancement in state service based on merit instead of the aristocratic privileges of the boyars. For its part, the merchant class sought to eliminate all competition from any other quarter in society. It wanted tax reform and protective regulations to bar the advantages enjoyed by foreign merchants.

The two classes agreed on the need for regulation of legal procedures. The courts should be closer to the populace and should provide better guarantees, particularly in cases against the powerful. Both merchants and landowners called for a return to the times when representatives of the district population took part in legal deliberations. They also concurred in protesting the privileged positions of clerical and secular lords, especially in matters of obligations to the crown and legal immunity. Step by step they urged the fulfillment of their demands, persisting in the face of stern opposition mounted against the social and political principles they advanced. The crown authorities retorted that "the chattels and servants of the sovereign have never decreed the actions of the grand sovereigns." In the opinion of the crown, the requests and demands exceeded the material needs of these groups. It rejected the notion of restoring the popular representation feature characteristic of the Assembly of the Land in provincial courts and administration, asserting that "never had there been a time when peasants sat with boyars, officials and governors to adjudicate legal matters, and no such time would ever come." The crown government mercilessly rebuffed the designs of representatives of social classes to gain the right of initiative in the Assembly of the Land and dismissed the protests of electors dismayed because their delegates were unable to include their "various whims in the law code."

The wishes of the middle social groups reached the government in abundance in the form of petitions to the Assemblies of the Land and by other means. The authorities themselves encouraged this by inviting to the assemblies all who "could describe violations, oppression and destruction," and promising to consider with the delegates all needs and deprivations of the population. The common goal would be the improvement of conditions in Muscovy in order that the economy might function at maximum capacity. Of these demands the crown met only those it considered necessary and beneficial to the interests of the sovereign and the realm. The elected delegates were relegated to the role of useful and knowledgeable subjects, but submissive petitioners nonetheless. As a result, the Assemblies of the Land did not become an organic part of Muscovy's political system.

DECLINE OF THE ASSEMBLY OF THE LAND

After providing essential support to Tsar Michael Romanov in his first years of rule in upholding the shaken authority of the central government, the Assembly of the Land declined in importance and became the voice of the land and of the class segments comprising it. The crown listened with apparent attentiveness but with increasing dissatisfaction. Criticism of the administrative chancellories sounded too stridently and complaints concerning the highest levels of rule were too prevalent in the 1640s to please the ear of the tsar. This produced severe anxiety and fear of popular disorders caused by discontent generated by the oppression practiced by crown officials and their burdensome enslavement of society as a whole. The attempt to refer the revolt in Pskov in 1650 to the Assembly of the Land had such unsatisfactory results that the authorities were forced to put under surveillance the "criminal" speeches that resounded throughout the very capital city of Moscow itself. The administration hurried to do away with the practice of national consultative sessions, and the Assemblies of the Land of the 1650s which dealt with the struggle for the Ukraine preserved merely the semblance rather than the substance of the institution. Members of the Assembly, now divided into classes, merely approved prior decisions of the tsar and his boyar council. The impotence of the Assembly is exemplified by the government response to a merchant appeal of 1660. The Muscovite merchants of various categories proclaimed that they could not address themselves to a question so important as the matter of providing funds to avoid a monetary crisis. This, they declared, was a matter for the entire country, for all cities and all classes. The government preferred to admit its bankruptcy openly rather than convene the Assembly of the Land.

THE BUREAUCRATIC IMPERATIVE

The brief period in which the Assembly of the Land functioned was a time of feverish bureaucratic development in the government. The assemblies remained nothing more than an extraordinary administrative device aimed at dealing with particularly vexing and difficult problems. Even so, the general conditions existing in Russia did not favor realignment of domestic political relationships. In the wake of the Time of Troubles, Moscow expended immense energies in restoring the social and political order that lay smashed beneath the ruins of the state. The circumstances of Russia's foreign relations merely increased the tension in Muscovy, injecting the urgent need for the more thorough subordination of domestic society and physical resources to the flowering requirements of the government. During the first decades of the rule of the new Romanov dynasty the Muscovite state succeeded in consolidating itself within the territorial boundaries drawn subsequent to the losses incurred during the Time of Troubles. This cost great exertion, but it was a time of rejuvenating and concentrating the might of the nation before beginning a new and aggressive leap outward.

Gradually the old Russian urge for expansion reappeared. Expeditions pushed toward the Baltic, the Dnieper basin and south to the Black Sea. Colonization flourished beyond the Volga and eastward to the Urals and the depths of Siberia. In the course of the seventeenth century a deep transformation settled over Moscow's international position. It brought with it a fundamental change in domestic policies as well. In subjugating the Ukraine, the Great Russian state began again to bring to life the "state of all the Russias." The tsardom of Muscovy was about to be transformed into the Russian Empire.

The initial stages of this metamorphosis involved territorial expansion that exceeded the governing capabilities of Moscow. A peculiar cultural and historical situation emerged in connection with the unusual ethnic complexities of the population of the enlarged state. Whereas the tsardom of Muscovy initially had blossomed in Great Russian soil, now it lost its ancient regional character. The organizational needs confronting the government increased drastically thanks to this general historical process. The expenditures required to sustain the daily costs of military and civilian administration were immense. In the seventeenth century, therefore, the bondage of society as a whole in service and taxation achieved far greater definition and finality. Accompanying this development was a much stricter differentiation between the various social classes. The social structure of Muscovite Russia presented the image of a harmonious system of stable and eternal serfdom in which the sovereign's subjects were assigned to four "great estates"—the clergy, the service nobility, the merchantry and the serfs. Their roles were clearly distinguished on the basis of responsibilities to the state as well as by special rights and activities. Of course, this idealized image corresponded poorly to reality. It can hardly be said that the population of Muscovy had crystallized so completely into fixed classes. Colonization and the growth of the national territory, as well as the primitive economic structure and the conditions of commerce and manufacturing, inhibited any such precise social differentiation, no matter how intensively the authorities cultivated it.

The efforts of the government to orient Muscovy's entire social structure toward service and tax obligations produced greater bureaucratic centralization and reliance on powerful administrative offices to guide local affairs. The seventeenth century brought with it the flourishing of autocratic rule and the departmental principle of administrative organization. The human and physical disarray created by the Time of Troubles, and the simple lack of resources in the face of the rapidly growing demands of government, made the need for a firm central administration more compelling than during the sixteenth century. The central authorities sought to concentrate in their hands full responsibility and control in all national affairs. The trend toward increased centralization found substance in the burgeoning bureaucratic institutions. After the Time of Troubles, Muscovy witnessed intensive efforts to revitalize the service estates and experienced much individual as well as state economic activity. Gradually attempts were made to solve the most pressing problems linked to new military, commercial and manufacturing developments, to master the technological advances of Western Europe in these fields, and to manage better the economic and cultural affairs of the country. To cast more broadly its administrative net, the central authorities established new government departments. In pursuing public affairs and the business of state their numbers increased, as did their influence. Patriarch Filaret[12] and Tsar Alexis, no less, grew disturbed at the independent power of the administrative departments, whose activities provoked popular consternation, and which were not always responsive to the wishes of the head of state.

The personal role of the tsar in matters of administration held but secondary importance. To officials and the population at large the tsar's own administrative activity customarily stood in the shadow of the presumptuous departmental bureaucracy. The tsar sought to combat this image by charging special institutions staffed with trusted persons to deal with the abuses, and in general, the entrenched procedures of the departments, which Tsar Alexis described irritably as the "sly customs of Moscow" and "Moscow red tape." As institutions of highest instance, the departments that processed petitions against the high and the mighty gained the color of extraordinary inspectorates and investigative agencies. Yet they offered little in the way of lasting results. Consequently, Tsar Alexis Mikhailovich, who insisted on participating personally in ruling the state, created a unique office outside and above the regular departmental structure, to carry out his will, called the "Sovereign's Department for Privy Affairs." It examined, acted on, followed and revised the widest variety of administrative matters. Any activity of particular interest to the tsar might be referred to this confidential office, whether a matter of personal interest or of principle.

MILITARY GOVERNORS

The mighty bureaucracy reached into local governmental institutions as well. Beginning immediately after the Time of Troubles, the government in Moscow undertook new arrangements in the provinces to bring all local institutions under the umbrella of the central administration. Despite the vitality acquired by the self-governing rural communities while the government recovered from collapse, Moscow did not turn to these existing bodies for support. Rather, it labored to strengthen the departmental form of provincial administration. A ready model for this approach was provided by an institution born of the war-torn and anxious circumstances of the Time of Troubles, the office of military governor. Previously these posts had existed only in the border regions where a constant threat was posed by the restless inhabitants, migrants and fugitives from central Russia requiring special vigilance. The military governors enjoyed a combination of military, financial and police authority; moreover, they conducted law courts and other arbitration covering the entire population. The conditions of the Time of Troubles had encouraged the appointment of military governors or commandants with similarly broad authority among the cities and districts of Muscovy's central regions. During the era of the Assemblies of the Land these governors frequently supervised the assemblies themselves. The new Romanov dynasty approved the military governors and utilized them throughout the realm to magnify official authority.

The military commandant or governor did not enjoy the status of independent appointed governor. Rather, it would be more accurate to say that he headed an office of the central departmental administration. His was the responsibility for executing the plethora of directives and regulations originating in Moscow. Nor was he an official paid and maintained by the local population. He transmitted incomes due the state directly and in full to the sovereign, and received no direct support from the populace. This highly rudimentary local government grew to be the nearly unmanageable master of the local population. Without information, with the general breakdown in order and the complex new demands of administering a growing territory, the central authorities found it imperative to grant to military governors an extremely broad and poorly defined authority. Although it desired to regulate their activities, the government held no option but to accept without consultation measures deemed appropriate to local conditions by the commandants themselves. Meanwhile, the government's lack of funds and capacity for organization forced the military commandants to rely on local populations for support, and with their subordinates to subsist on the "voluntary" contributions of their charges. Neither the government nor the public found fault with this situation. The crafty customs of the departmental bureaucracies poisoned the central administration and local government equally, having become an entrenched feature of the cultural and material poverty of Muscovite Russia.

It was with these elementary forms of government that the tsardom of Muscovy during the seventeenth century faced the enormously complex problems of its international and domestic situation.

CHAPTER ELEVEN

THE TSARDOM OF MUSCOVY

THE CHARACTER OF MUSCOVY

In the 1660s the tsardom of Muscovy was studied carefully by a visitor, the Croatian Catholic priest Yury Krizhanich.[1] The first Pan-Slavist, Krizhanich had dreamed of mighty Muscovy, the future liberator of the Slavs from foreign domination. He fancied the unification of the Slavs on the foundations of their common political interests and cultural life as Slavs and Catholics.[2] The crucial point of departure for these reveries was the administrative, economic and cultural flourishing of the Muscovite state.

The reality he found in Moscow totally disillusioned the Croatian dreamer. His observations convinced him that the only active creative force in Russia was the absolute autocracy. Untrammelled by any numerous assaults on its supreme power, the autocracy might direct national life rationally and transcend clashing class interests. Strong government might regulate social relationships, establish useful and just laws, legal procedures and consistent administrative practices while developing commerce and manufacturing and promoting that enlightenment which would answer the longings of the Russian people. But all this lay in the future. Krizhanich personally was an advocate of enlightened absolutism. He was animated by faith in the creative power and capabilities of the state and the human intellect, and he looked with bold confidence to the future, despite the depressing situation around him.

The realities of Russian life made of Krizhanich a severe and observant critic. The autocratic rule which he valued so highly existed in a distorted and perverted form in Russia. Arbitrary rule had transformed Muscovy into a tsardom of tyranny and governance by bad laws. Absolutism had ruined the land thanks to its short-sighted financial system; it had perverted the people through its alcohol monopoly and demeaned it through capricious rule. Official laxity corrupted the Muscovite administration by condescendingly permitting the abuses of the bureaucracy while forcing its officials to seek their livelihood through graft and bribery because of wretched salaries. The very approach to administration which made treasury interests paramount led to the extraction of the last penny from the people, with no thought for the public good.

The overall style of life in Muscovy corrupted the people as well. They lived in poverty and ignorance, doing nothing according to conscience but always in fear of punishment. They were schooled to deceit and sloth. To Krizhanich, these sins and misfortunes of Russian life found their historical explanations in the principles of harsh rule and human exploitation imposed by Ivan the Terrible, not only because of his own nature but also as a consequence of his preoccupation with war and foreign struggle. His reign quickly was followed by the interregnum and its troubles, which finally destroyed the edifice of state. When at last the new dynasty arrived, it needed first of all to restore and bolster the outward form of governance. Only when that was accomplished might it begin to refurbish the methods of government by enacting new legislation. A typical rationalist, Krizhanich explained these features of Russian life as the fruits of evil laws; reasonable legislation would provide remedies for the shortcomings of government and popular vices. Harsh rule likewise was to blame for Russia's sparse population, in Krizhanich's opinion, as well as for the country's poorly developed economic order and low cultural level. Actually, Krizhanich mistook cause for effect; echoing the world view of his times, he wanted to sweep the staircase from the bottom while building it from the top. At the same time, he was correct in his understanding of the tasks confronting the Russian authorities. His projects for sweeping reforms coincided with fundamental trends in Muscovy's official life.

INTERNATIONAL IMPERATIVES

The tsardom of Muscovy had been nourished by the soil of Great Russia, but after the middle of the sixteenth century it had burst from its confines onto the broad expanses of the East European steppes. The Great Russian people pressed colonization ever forward while the Muscovite state strained to master the steppe by ceaselessly and aggressively expanding the frontiers, to the west, south and east simultaneously. Without access in the West to the sea, the challenge of building a better economic order and national culture could not be met. The impossible burdens heaped on the Muscovite peasantry produced an exodus to the south, to the rich black soils and vast steppes with their untouched wealth. That elemental military and economic colonization of the Don region by free Great Russian cossacks drew after it the arm of Muscovite government, which inexorably turned from defending the southern frontier toward implacable advances, ever southward. The southern border with the Tatar peoples of the steppes long had been an exhausting nightmare for Great Russia. Constantly exposed to enemy forays and eternally uneasy, the frontier demanded sleepless observation and protection. Each year the unexpected attacks of the Crimean Tatars required troop movements to the south. Permanent outposts and guard stations had to be maintained, with border fortresses, ramparts and barriers erected to form lines of advance defensive positions. The defense of the country consumed amounts of men and resources no less vast than any actual war.

By the middle of the seventeenth century several major fortification projects were completed to fill out an unbroken line of defense in the south and southeast, stretching from the town of Akhtyrka on the Vorskla river to Ufa. While the integrity of that restless border was greatly improved, the battles in the south did not come to an end. That they persisted so long clearly signaled the urgency of conquering the steppe as far as the Black Sea to preserve a semblance of order on the southern border lands. Other political and geographic considerations endemic in Great Russia pointed to the same conclusion. The perennial struggle for Smolensk with the Lithuanians, and gradual advances in the north, were developments as similar in importance to the northeastern Muscovite heartland as the press into the Dnieper basin, whither long-standing colonial and national economic motivations drew Great Russia. During the Time of Troubles Moscow had lost these regions. The urge to repossess them was an elemental force rather than a political ambition. Moreover, access to the southern routes to the Black Sea was blocked without mastery of the Dnieper basin.

The domestic crisis in the Commonwealth of Lithuania, rekindled by Bohdan Khmelnitsky's revolt,[3] brought the problem to a head. Muscovy had been actively waging a protracted battle to master the Ukraine. A temporary resolution of the southern question was achieved by the Andrusovo truce and the treaty of "eternal peace" with Poland in 1686. The urge to the south introduced Muscovy into the broad new arena of international affairs in the Near East. By the end of the seventeenth century Russia was involved in its first war with Turkey, and a new era opened which would dominate its foreign affairs throughout the next century.

It was during this same period also that the Great Russian colonization of the eastern frontier began. The first quarter of the seventeenth century found Russians penetrating the vast territories beyond the Kama river and down the Volga. The need to establish peace and order there to protect new settlements and commercial routes to Asia led the Muscovite authorities to stage long and bitter campaigns against the restless tribes of those areas. Russia was drawn ever deeper into the basin of the Caspian Sea, along the pathways that later were to shape imperial policies toward Central Asia. Waves of migrations of Russians seeking a better economic life and new commerce carried Russia's pioneers into Siberia and toward the Far East. During the reign of Tsar Michael Romanov, Russians reached the shores of the Sea of Okhotsk and began settling the banks of the Yenisey and Lena rivers. In the 1640s Russian settlers became entrenched in the Anadyrsky region, in the Trans-Baikal region, and penetrated to the Amur river. By the year 1689 a treaty with China provided the first definite limitation on further expansion into the Far East.[4]

Rapidly broadening political horizons fed the quest for new sources of national enrichment and culture. The Muscovite state grew steadily more enmeshed in international commerce, attracting foreigners into transit arrangements for trade with East Asia, and developing ties with Europe. The noble A.L. Ordin-Nashchokin[5] suggested that now Moscow's most important priority should be the acquisition of Livonia and a seacoast in the west. The lure of an open sea route on the Baltic motivated Tsar Alexis to concentrate his efforts on solving the Baltic question, while neglecting the Ukraine and conquests in Western Russia. Whereas it merely had loomed on the European scene at the end of the sixteenth century, Muscovy in the seventeenth century belonged fully to the community of European states.

CRISIS AND GOVERNANCE

But by that time Muscovy was no longer the same. The Great Russian heartland was now merely the focal point of the transformation of the tsardom of Muscovy into a vast empire. Consequently, the very foundations of Russian life experienced a deep-running and complex crisis in the seventeenth century. Suffering the piercing pangs of historical labor, Muscovy gave birth to a new Russia. The country survived this crisis and overcame it only at the pain of an extraordinary organizational effort. The strained socio-political order, shackled by general enserfment, the growing administrative centralization, and the bureaucratization of all institutions, nonetheless continued to mature within the confines imposed on it by the government. With the passage of time greater efforts had to be invested in resolving problems not directly related to Great Russian national affairs. The steadily expanding territory and the increasingly varied ethnic composition of the realm brought an immense shift in the national amalgam. The Great Russian state was reborn as the Russian Empire, a multi-national state in which the Russian element comprised merely the foundation and cohesive force. But it was Great Russia which had fused and assimilated these diverse elements. The seventeenth century was a period of transition which culminated in the formal shift of Russian political life from the Great Russian center of Moscow to St. Petersburg, the seat of the Russian Empire.

The multi-faceted crisis which wrenched the Muscovite state during the seventeenth century was accompanied by a noticeable firming of governance and enhanced mastery over every turn of national life. The government's active tutelage of the Russian people grew markedly. But once it had instituted new and harsher methods of exploiting population and natural resources in the service of the state, the crown found itself face to face with some very clear consequences of its policies. The measures imposed had proven to be gravely inadequate, and there was urgent need for rapid improvement and development. Thus, although the ideas of Yury Krizhanich reflected theoretical views drawn from the political writings of the Catholic West, they also revealed a perceptive grasp of Russian realities which gave sure confirmation to theory.

Absolute monarchy in Muscovy reached full maturity during the course of the extreme crisis experienced throughout the entire gamut of official and public affairs. The accepted traditions of intellectual and everyday life rapidly decayed and disappeared, and social relationships were shaken and distorted.

The powerful initiatives of the government met no resistance from any well-organized public groups, or by an definite, consistent public opinion. The crown found itself the master of the destiny of the country and of all classes of the population, responsible solely to God as the preceptor of the material and spiritual life of Muscovy.

As the annointed of God, the tsar stood high above the country. Such was the opinion of Tsar Alexis. The tsar's high measures were governed by divine providence, and the sayings "the tsar's heart is in God's hands" and "God will guide and inform the tsar" were taken at face value when decisions were made in important matters. Tsar Alexis believed firmly in his divinely established and even divinely inspired authority, even though he was prepared to admit with Christian humility that he personally in his human limitations was not worthy to be, in the earthly life of God's people, "the great sun, or even a small beacon." On the other hand, he demanded from the servants of the tsar a total, reverent obedience, "in fear of God and the sovereign." His rebuke of a boyar for insubordination to a sovereign decree echos like a reproach for a religious sin: "Whom are you not obeying? Christ himself!" Although personally sensitive and attentive to the needs of others, Tsar Alexis sharply rejected all demands upon the sovereign by his subjects, whether by public protest against the oppression of the administrative bureaucracy or by personal requests, for example, for deserved rewards. The tsar's "resolve was evident in all such matters, even in the granting of just petitions, but for those who petitioned with reproach there was rejection of all demands." The servants of the sovereign held no rights before the supreme ruler. The tsar's grace was the sole source of those perquisites they considered to be rights. Tsar Alexis' idealized version of sovereign power coincided with the popular view that the tsar was the fountain of highest justice in formal as well as practical everyday matters. Individual petitions flowed to the tsar personally in the hope of circumventing departmental obfuscation and the contradictions between statutory rights and practical justice. The sovereign received complaints of abuses and oppression practiced by low-ranking officials, and his terrible "word and deed" were invoked to attract the crown's attention to excesses. The sovereign's subjects sought his protection because they held no civil rights, a fact directly attributable to the bureaucratic barricade between the central government and the people. The tsar of the seventeenth century shared these popular views and expressed his consternation about the crafty practices of the departments, and from time to time he attempted to establish closer supervision of the administrative authorities and to inflict harsh penalties for their vicious crimes. The consequences of the bureaucratic system and the conditions in which it functioned were ethical and moral bankruptcy and lack of discipline. On the other hand, the dream of social justice found incarnation in the religious and moral idealization of the sovereign, and the legend grew.

The myth of the benevolent tsar became a characteristic feature of popular risings, which were directed against the boyars and government administrative officials. Concerning the tsar, on the other hand, popular sayings in restless times declared that "the present tsar is merciful, and will drive the mighty from the tsardom. Let us beat the powerful villains with staff and cudgel." When rebuking the sovereign, the popular sayings claimed that he "saw everything through the mouths of his boyars," and that "he could not alone wreak retribution in the land, for his people guided him."

The entire history of Muscovite absolutism reflects the struggle between personal autocratic power and its usurpation by bureaucratic government institutions. The ancient monarchy grew convinced that all governmental evil flowed from bureaucratic oppression, and that the cure lay in the supralegal intervention of the sovereign, who alone was untouched by the dead hand of formalism. Only gradually did the aspiration to subordinate official institutions to principles of legality to achieve orderly government reveal that the real threat to this high purpose lay in absolutist rule, which diametrically contravened true legality. But the seventeenth century was still far from any such understanding. Meanwhile the tsar's government enjoyed an unprecedented flourishing of its autocracy, expansion of its activities, and intensification of its control over national life. Thanks to brute strength and the bureaucratic hierarchy it weathered the sullen thunder and stormy explosions of the Russian people's elemental protest against the burdens of serfdom.

CULTURE AND CRISIS

The ideology of the Muscovite state during the reign of Tsar Alexis continued to infuse the concept and purposes of state authority with religious and moral principles. This was the time of the last, dying flourish of the medieval world view. Underlying Muscovy's entry onto the broad stage of international affairs was Alexis' understanding of the historical notion of Moscow's significance to the Christian world. As the "third Rome" the Russian capital was viewed as the final seat of the universal, ideal Christian empire and the last bastion of the true, orthodox and universal faith. Alexis associated religious motives with all questions of both domestic and international policies. A.L. Ordin-Nashchokin's political argument against the struggle for the Ukraine in favor of a single-minded commitment to reach the Baltic met the tsar's resistance. In the latter's view, it was improper and even sinful to abandon the "Circassian matter"[6] of liberating an Orthodox land from the rule of infidels. In international affairs Moscow was called to lead the Orthodox East in staunchly resisting the heterodox West and the world of Islam. Divine providence inspired in the tsar the strength necessary for him to shepherd God's own people in the ways of justice based on morality, religious precepts and the true faith.

The theocratic bent of the tsarist government found expression in Tsar Alexis' numerous letters and decrees, rich in

religious admonitions and ethical maxims. They strongly colored relations between the Muscovite state and the Russian
church. Patriarch Nikon[7] attempted to exalt spiritual authority,
to hold it in independence of secular power and to portray the
patriarch as the "image of Christ." As supreme pastor and "ultimate father," his authority was unconditional and unques-
tionable. He declared that his office ordained him to "proclaim
the teachings of God and the rules of the church." The outcome was conflict between the two rivals for power. The church
council held in 1667 condemned Nikon, but decided the basic
question of church autonomy in favor of the clergy, and declared that "the tsar holds primacy in civil matters, whereas
the patriarch reigns supreme in church affairs." The tsar refused
to accept the council's decision, and removed it from the official acts of the council.

The provisional outcome of this conflict brought government victory over the church. The ultimate consequences of
the struggle between church and state came half a century later,
when the patriarchate was abolished and replaced by the so-
called "ruling synod," the official institution exercising secular control of church affairs. The tragedy of the Russian church
was of far-reaching importance for the cultural crisis in Muscovite Russia. This was so because of the clash of competing cultural influences at that historical moment. The Western European currents typical of Protestant, Germanic nations turbu-
lently collided with the Ukrainian and Polish Catholic traditions,
which were closer to official Russian religiosity. Uncertainties
therefore found their way into the traditional way of life and
accepted outlooks on life. Fueled by the crises saturating national life, this general uncertainty drove a wedge between the
religious consciousness and the secular sphere of Russian existence. Stormily and painfully Russia underwent an assault on
its accustomed attitudes toward life. Powerful Catholic influences altered the theological conceptions and the aspirations of
the church hierarchy, and the divergence in beliefs brought the

schism in the Russian church that resulted in the emergence of
the official, Nikonian, state church, and numerous popular "old
believer" sects.[8] Now a new schism, fed by the altered relationships in society, built up between church and state, between
the old religious faith and the new secular social order. Yet,
deep within the bosom of the tsardom of Muscovy, where the
medieval mind still surrounded the sovereign and his high co-
horts, the secular view of state and political life grew irrepres-
sibly.

Clearly, the undertakings of the Muscovite state had grown
too complex and too urgent to permit the continued workings
of outmoded methods. Thus the acquisition of foreign military,
commercial and manufacturing skills, and such major innovations as shipbuilding, medical practice and postal communications soon were followed by credit procedures and regulation
of trade as means of influencing economic life. Finally, extreme
measures were required to satisfy the pressing demands of the
persons who had been prepared to perform sophisticated duties
in administration and economic life. Together these new trends
in state administration transformed Muscovy into a secular police state. These departures in the direction and structure of
governance paralleled and closely interacted with the sweeping
changes then suffusing the public and intellectual horizons of
the Russian people. A flood of novel and unprecedented impressions came to shape attitudes and outlooks on life. They
fostered different thought processes and created a need for fresh
resources and methods of expression. Engulfed as it was by a
wave of new cultural insights, Muscovy experienced a violent
break with established traditions which hastened their distortion
and decline. As this process advanced, fueled by the same secular set of values which·was transforming the state, it inspired
private manners and intellectual life. The old culture decayed
and disintegrated, and old Muscovite Russia lay dying. A different Russia stepped forward to take its place.

NOTES

Notes relating to specific Russian terminology are taken largely from the *Dictionary of Russian Historical Terms from the Eleventh Century to 1917*, compiled by Sergei G. Pushkarev and edited by George Vernadsky and Ralph T. Fisher, Jr. (Yale, 1970). Readers with a need for more comprehensive discussions of such terminology are referred to that source. For authoritative treatment of many topics and individuals mentioned in the text, see the appropriate entries in Joseph L. Wieczynski, ed., *The Modern Encyclopedia of Russian and Soviet History* (MERSH), Vol. 1 and following. Gulf Breeze: Academic International Press, 1976-.

INTRODUCTION

1. Poland's Jagellonian princes originated from Iagailo or Jagiello, son of the Lithuanian ruler Olgerd. Jagiello became king of Poland after converting to Catholicism, and ruled 1386-1434 as Wladyslaw II. See George Vernadsky, *The Mongols and Russia* (New Haven, 1951), pp. 238-240.

2. The Polish-Lithuanian Commonwealth formed at the end of the fourteenth century when Lithuania was absorbed into Poland to carry on the struggle against the Teutonic Knights. See Vernadsky, *The Mongols and Russia*, p. 240.

3. Grand Prince Ivan III the Great reigned 1462-1505. The decline of the Golden Horde's power accelerated significantly during his reign, whether his policies contributed greatly to the process or not. See Michael T. Florinsky, *Russia: A History and an Interpretation*, Vol. 1, pp. 68-70.

4. George Trachaniot's important mission for Russia typifies the special role played by Greek emigres throughout Southeastern and Eastern Europe, particularly in the lands following Orthodox Christian dogma, in the medieval period.

5. The Tatar Golden Horde played a central part in Russian history from the sacking of Kiev under Khan Batu in the thirteenth century until its gradual decline in the late fifteenth century. See Florinsky, *Russia*, pp. 56 ff.

6. Novgorod the Great, one of several cities with the name Novgorod in medieval Russia, traced its prominence to the legendary Varangian or Scandinavian ruler Rurik, who is said to have come there as prince in the ninth century. The merchant and aristocratic population of the city developed an oligarchic government and considerable liberty, which lasted until it was subdued by Muscovy in the mid-fifteenth century.

See *The Chronicle of Novgorod*, 1016-1471 (Hattiesburg: Academic International Press, 1970), vii-lx.

7. The Byzantine heritage was central for Russian culture after Prince Vladimir accepted the Greek form of Christianity in Kiev in 988. See George P. Majeska, "Byzantine Influence on Russia," MERSH, Vol. 6, pp. 74-80, and Walter K. Hanak, "Byzantine-Russian Relations," MERSH, Vol. 6, pp. 80-86.

CHAPTER ONE

1. The term Great Russia (Velikorossiia) is used generally to distinguish the central Russian areas from the Ukraine, called Malorossiia or Little Russia, and Byelorussia or White Russia.

2. Vladimir Monomakh, the son of Vsevolod, ruled Kievan Russia, or Rus', 1113-1125. The name Monomakh comes from his Greek mother. His accession was contested; after his death Kiev's prominence faded rapidly. See Florinsky, *Russia*, pp. 29-30.

3. Yury Dolgoruky (George the Long-Arm), a prince of Rostov, vied with Prince Iziaslav for control of Kiev. He is said to have founded the village which grew to become Moscow, in 1147.

4. Andrei Bogoliubsky, son of Yury Dolgoruky, reigned 1157-1174 in the northern center then called Rostov-Suzdal. His armies overran Kiev in 1169. Since he did not then move to the city, Kiev's decline was emphasized by his neglect of the former capital. See David M. Goldfrank, "Andrei Bogoliubskii," MERSH, Vol. 1, pp. 218-221.

5. Boyar (boiar): the general term for the high-ranking nobility of Russia from Kievan times. With the passage of time the basis of their prominence gradually shifted from land ownership toward service distinction. See Robert O. Crummey, "Boiar," MERSH, Vol. 5, pp. 49-51.

6. Prince (kniaz), appanage prince (udelnyi kniaz): the lands and populations inherited by a member of a ruling family of princes were called an appanage (udel) in the thirteenth-sixteenth centuries, and the aristocratic landholder an appanage prince or simply a prince. This system gradually was replaced by a service-oriented grant system for landholding.

7. Vladimir and Suzdal became the Russian cultural centers as the political focal point slowly shifted toward Moscow. The grand duchy, or principality, of Vladimir, with its vast resources, became the power base for the emerging Muscovite state. See Florinsky, *Russia*, pp. 89-91.

8. Vsevolod III, "The Big Nest," reigned 1176-1212 in Rostov-Suzdal. He sought, as had his predecessors, to subjugate Novgorod. The sobriquet presumably comes from his numerous important descendants.

9. Governor, appointed governor (namestnik): a crown governor, often a boyar. He was appointed by the grand prince, but his subsistence generally came directly from the local populations.

10. Military governor, military leader, or commandant (voevoda): originally the voevoda had clearly military responsibilities, but with the passage of time two important changes took place in the office. It became a suitable commission to grant to a former independent prince, thereby honoring him while subordinating him to the central authority. Secondly, the military leader's responsibilities broadened in scope and became those of a military governor, charged with preserving civil order as well as military readiness. Usage in the text reflects the evolution of responsibilities.

11. As early as the thirteenth century the Livonian German knights and the Swedes had threatened Novgorod and the Russian North. The threat posed by the German knights persisted until the reign of Ivan the Terrible in the second half of the sixteenth century, and that of the Swedes until the early eighteenth century. See George P. Majeska, "Alexander Nevskii," MERSH, Vol. 1, pp. 148-152.

12. See Edward D. Sokol, "Batu Khan," MERSH, Vol. 3, pp. 163-165.

13. In the two-front, unequal struggle of Russia against Swedes and Lithuanians in the west and Tatars in the east, Alexander Nevsky (reigned 1253-1263) holds a special place of honor for repelling the western aggressors. The exigencies of practical politics, however, seemed to demand submission to the Golden Horde. See George P. Majeska, "Alexander Nevskii," MERSH, Vol. 1, pp. 148-152.

14. The metropolitanate directed the Russian Orthodox Church from its inception until the highest church officer was elevated to patriarch under Boris Godunov, with the reluctant approval of the Byzantine hierarchy. See Florinsky, *Russia*, pp. 222-223.

15. Ivan Kalita, who reigned 1325-1341, collaborated with the Golden Horde. As partial reward he received the Grand Duchy of Vladimir in addition to his original principality of Moscow, thus laying the foundation for the Russian state. The epithet *Kalita* (moneybags) attached to his name recalls either his wealth or stinginess. See Florinsky, *Russia*, p. 87.

16. Scribes and chroniclers have provided virtually the only written records of Russia's early history. The chronicles they wrote are pious and terse, so that the information left for posterity is sometimes sparse. See, for example, Samuel H. Cross, the *Russian Primary Chronicle*, Cambridge, Mass., 1953; and *The Chronicle of Novgorod*, 1016-1471.

17. The Lithuanian Russian state refers to the political absorption of western Russian principalities by Lithuania in the thirteenth and fourteenth centuries. See Vernadsky, *The Mongols and Russia*, pp. 237-238.

18. Grand Prince Semen Ivanovich, also known as Semen the Proud, was the son of Ivan Kalita. He reigned 1341-1353, and died of the plague. See Vernadsky, *The Mongols and Russia*, pp. 237-238.

CHAPTER TWO

1. Rural district (volost), rural district administrator (volostel), rural district council or peasant commune (volostnoi mir): an administrative subdivision below the *uezd* level with considerable autonomous authority for managing economic affairs. The rural district official was appointed by the central government.

2. Elder of a village (zemskii starosta): an elected leader of a rural district commune. Elected elders played major roles throughout provincial government.

3. Service and dues payment obligations (tiaglo), taxpaying population (tiagloe naselenie): originally the term *tiaglo* indicated a labor obligation which the general population was responsible for through rural district organizations and the like. Later, certain classes of the populace were exempted from such taxation because of other services they provided, or were supposed to provide, to the central government. These included the service nobility, the clergy, and certain strata of the merchantry. Often as well, the serfs of manorial estates did not pay any sums directly to the crown, but only to their master. The remaining population was obliged to contribute money to the treasuries of the crown.

4. Lord lieutenant, that is, appointed governor (namestnik). See note 9, Chapter One.

5. Constable (dovodchik): an executive agent, or bailiff, of district officials or governors.

6. Maintenance (kormlenie), maintained boyars or governors (kormlenshchiki): the system in which appointed officials received their subsistence and other benefits directly from the local populations they were sent to govern. Originally the maintenance was delivered in kind, but eventually it became monetary payments.

CHAPTER THREE

1. The "Russian land" is the earliest name for the Kievan Russian state and was a term of ideological legitimacy in the Muscovite period. See Charles J. Halperin, "The Concept of the Russian Land from the Ninth to the Fourteenth Centuries," *Russian History*, II, Part 1 (1975), pp. 29-38.

2. Grand prince of all Russia (velikii kniaz vseia Rusi): the traditional term from Kievan times for the senior prince; it continued in use to stress the prince's legitimate right to power.

3. The Danilovich family was connected to Daniil of Moscow, who reigned as prince in 1261-1303.

4. Advice and counsel (duma i sgadtsa): a term applied to consultations between princes to assist in deciding the general policies of

of the grand principality as well as common action to execute such policies.

5. Dmitry Donskoi, Grand Prince of Moscow 1350-1389, led the famous Russian victory over the Tatars at Kulikovo field. The geographic location, beyond the Don River, provided Dmitry's title and served as the name for the famous epic poem on the Russian victory, the *Zadonshchina*. See Vernadsky, *The Mongols and Russia*, pp. 259-262.

6. Service nobility (sluzhilyi klass): in place of the original hereditary landholding nobility of princes and boyars there gradually developed an aristocracy which owed its status and lands to the grants of the sovereign grand prince, and later, of the tsar. These grants were rewards for services, and might be temporary or permanent in nature.

7. For an example of Ivan Kalita's practices in purchasing estates from his service nobility, see Vernadsky, *Russia at the Dawn of the Modern Age*, p. 111.

8. Vasily the Dark, or the Blind, was grand prince 1425-1462. The sobriquet attached to his name refers to the fact that in 1446 he was blinded in a domestic dispute. Vasily ultimately prevailed despite his disability. See Florinsky, *Russia*, pp. 68-69.

9. Servitor (volnyi sluga, sluzhilyi): a previously free noble who voluntarily agreed to enter the service of a prince in return for rewards of land and status. As this practice grew the service nobility emerged from it.

10. Vasily III, reigned 1503-1533. He was the father of Ivan IV the Terrible. See Sergei M. Soloviev, *History of Russia*, Vol. 9: *The Age of Vasily III*. Edited and translated by Hugh F. Graham. Gulf Breeze: Academic International Press, 1976.

11. Ivan IV, or Ivan the Terrible, was the first Russian ruler officially crowned as tsar, or emperor. While the Russian term *grozny* attached to his name has respectful connotations of awe and dread, the usual translation of "The Terrible" seems to characterize his reign successfully. See S.F. Platonov, *Ivan the Terrible*. Gulf Breeze: Academic International Press, 1974.

12. Ivan Ivanovich, the son of Ivan III, should naturally have provided the heir to the principality. Such violations of the succession as described here, however, are typical rather than exceptional for Russian dynastic politics.

13. The Byzantine princess Sofia Paleologus was the niece of the last emperor of Byzantium before it fell to the Turks in 1453. According to Vernadsky, her marriage to Ivan III legitimized a Russian claim to the Byzantine legacy if it could be recovered. See *The Mongols and Russia*, p. 385.

14. Tsar (tsar): Presniakov takes rather little note of the change in title from grand prince to tsar (caesar) for the Russian sovereign. Ivan IV was the first officially crowned tsar, although the term had been applied to Ivan III.

CHAPTER FOUR

1. Commune or peasant commune (mir): a rural body for self-rule, charged with maintaining public order, managing local civil and land affairs, and paying taxes. There were few formal guidelines or limitations on the activities of the mir.

2. Retinue (druzhina); retainer (kniazhii or "svoi" chelovek. [man] pl. liudi): the retinue dates back to the Kievan period, when it included the close circle of lords-in-waiting, courtiers and battle leaders around the prince. This institution had its counterpart in Muscovy in the nobles who served the princes, and the grand prince, personally.

3. Michael of Tver vied with Yury of Moscow for supremacy by seeking the khan's approval as grand prince. Michael's endeavors were continued by his successor Michael II of Tver in the late fourteenth century. See Vernadsky, *The Mongols and Russia*, pp. 193-194, 252-255, 265-268.

4. The authenticity of the epic *The Tale of Igor's Campaign* has been debated since its rediscovery in the early nineteenth century. See Vladimir Nabokov's careful and witty, but sometimes fanciful, translation and commentary (New York, 1960).

5. Petition (chelobit'e): a request to the grand prince or tsar, characterized by the ritual of presentation involving prostration before the sovereign, dating from Mongol times.

6. Lesser gentry (deti boiarskie and dvoriane): landholding and service nobles of medium rank; see also note 15 below.

7. Sergei M. Soloviev and Vasily O. Kliuchevsky were the most prominent Russian prerevolutionary historians. Kliuchevsky's *Kurs russkoi istorii* (A Course of Russian History) has been reprinted several times and imperfectly translated into English. Soloviev's magnum opus runs to 29 volumes: *Istoriia Rossii s drevneishikh vremen* (The History of Russia from Earliest Times). An English-language edition of the latter work is in progress by Academic International Press.

8. Department or office (put): these divisions for administration of the affairs of the prince or grand prince were entrusted with such matters as control of the stables, the larder, the hunting equipment, and land utilization. They gradually became more institutionalized, then evolved into the *prikazy* or bureaus which later administered the prince's affairs.

9. Lesser boyars (deti boiarskie or "boyar children"): these members of the boyar aristocracy might actually be the sons of boiars, but more often the term referred to gentry with smaller estates and lower aristocratic genealogies. The lesser boyars could aspire to and rise to greater station.

10. The Kievan period of Russian history extended from the ninth century to the earlier twelfth century. It saw the arrival of Christianity, brought by Prince Vladimir in 988 from Byzantium. After a time of

considerable international prestige under Yaroslav the Wise, Vsevolod, and Vladimir Monomakh, Kiev fell to the Tatars and its golden age ended.

11. Commons (ugodia): the forests and fields that were not divided up for cultivation in medieval Russia, but were available for hunting, fishing, and pasture, with permission of the local authorities.

12. Presniakov does not give citations for his quotations from the works of Kliuchevsky and other scholars.

13. Land grants, grant charters (zhalovannaia gramota): the prince's device for rewarding those who served him; there were several forms, ranging from permanent grants to temporary and partial disbursements from the excess income of a particular estate.

14. Fief (pomest'e, pomestnaia sistema): the practice of granting small provincial estates in return for service, including military terms; it produced the provincial gentry (pomeshchiki).

15. Serfs (krestiane or Christians): a term which emerged from the concept of the general Christian population. With growing enslavement, the notion of bondage or serfdom replaced that of free agricultural laboring peasants.

16. For a discussion of service oaths, see Soloviev, *History of Russia.* Vol. 9: *The Age of Vasily III*, pp. 120-121.

17. Baron Sigismund Herberstein provided a lasting source of impressions of Russia. His original work was in Latin; a Russian translation appeared in St. Petersburg in 1908 as *Zapiski o moskovitskikh delakh* (Notes of the Affairs of Muscovy). The best-known English translation is by R.H. Major, *Notes upon Russia*, 2 vols., London, 1851-1852.

CHAPTER FIVE

1. Tarkhan grant (tarkhan): a document granting exemption from taxes and/or placing the recipient directly under the tutelage of the grand prince.

2. Kliuchevsky's *Boiarskaia duma drevnei Rusi* (The Boyar Council of Ancient Russia) saw many editions, for example, Moscow, 1907.

3. Vladimir Monomakh's "Statute on Interest Payments" is a common term for an article of the expanded *Russkaia Pravda* (The Russian Law). See Vernadsky, *Medieval Russian Laws* (New York, 1947), pp. 43 ff.

4. *The Law Code (Sudebnik) of 1497* is found in *Sudebniki XV-XVI vekov* (Law Codes of the Fifteenth-Sixteenth Centuries), edited by B.D. Grekov (Moscow-Leningrad, 1952). Commentaries include that of Marc Szeftel in *For Roman Jakobson* (The Hague, 1956), pp. 547-552. For a translation of Ivan the Terrible's law code, see Horace W. Dewey, *Muscovite Judicial Texts, 1488-1556* (Michigan Slavic Materials, 7: Ann Arbor, 1966), pp. 7-21.

5. N.I. Lange was a legal historian.

6. Grand Prince Vasily I Dmitrievich, son of Dmitry Donskoi, reigned 1389-1425. He sought to build on his father's victory, but was generally unsuccessful. See Florinsky, *Russia*, pp. 66-67; Vernadsky, *The Mongols and Russia*, pp. 284-287. For a translation of the Dvina charter referred to in this passage, see Vernadsky, *Medieval Russian Laws*, pp. 57-60.

7. The boyars can be contrasted to the princes in that the former were hereditary aristocrats without obligation to the princes or the grand prince for their estates. This meant considerable independence; the boyars thus sought to advise and counsel the prince from a position of power. On the other hand, the princes of Russia originated as a family, or clan, with a senior authoritative member. Though the principle was often violated, obedience to the eldest prince was a matter of filial respect.

8. Palace boyars or inner circle of boyars (vvedennye boyare): those high ranking nobles who were councillors of the grand prince, and part of his court's entourage.

9. Boyar council (boiarskaia duma): a customary rather than legally constituted advisory body to the princes and later, the tsars of Russia.

10. State council: Presniakov uses the term *gosudarstvennaia duma* here but apparently it is the same as the boyar council, his usual term.

11. Prince Andrei Kurbsky, an important dissenter in the time of Ivan the Terrible, is best remembered because of his brief but unique correspondence with the first tsar. After departing Moscow to join the forces of Lithuania, Kurbsky wrote harsh criticism of Ivan's failure to consult with the boyars as he ruled the realm. Ivan replied in abusive terms intended to discourage further overt insubordination by the Russian boyars. See J.L.I. Fennell, ed. and trans., *The Correspondence Between Prince A.M. Kurbsky and Tsar Ivan IV of Russia*, 1564-1579 (Cambridge, 1963) and Platonov, *Ivan the Terrible*.

12. *The Discourse of the Miracle-Workers of Valaam* and the commentary referred to by Presniakov are literary and polemical works of the sixteenth century.

13. Saint Vladimir, that is, Prince Vladimir I of Kiev, was canonized for bringing Christianity to Kievan Russia and for his secular leadership.

14. Alexis Mikhailovich was the second Romanov tsar, reigning 1645-1676. During his reign Russian cultural ferment and state power advanced rapidly, setting the stage for the reforms of his famous son, Peter the Great. See Joseph T. Fuhrmann, "Aleksei Mikhailovich," MERSH, Vol. 1, pp. 115-120.

15. The institution of the *oprichnina* served Ivan the Terrible for establishing his rule and disposing of his enemies, brutally and thoroughly. The term initially referred to a special domain exempted from general state administration, and controlled directly by the tsar. From this privileged territory's populace, Ivan IV recruited an elite force marked by

two symbols, a dog's head showing that they would tear at the throat of all opposition, and a broom, as they would sweep away all opposition to Ivan. Cf. Florinsky, *Russia*, pp. 199-202, and Platonov, *Ivan the Terrible*, pp. 79 ff.

16. Customs of the land (zemskaia starina): procedures, practices and attributes of rural life and self-government organization that built up over centuries and frequently acquired the force of common law.

CHAPTER SIX

1. Olgerd of Lithuania (d. 1377) gained the epithet "fire worshipper" because he was regarded as a pagan. Vernadsky suggests that in fact he may have become Greek Orthodox. In any case, he was a powerful ruler of the Lithuanian state at its zenith, when it controlled most of what is now the Ukraine. See Vernadsky, *The Mongols and Russia*, pp. 237-241.

2. The reports of the Englishman Chancellor, rewritten by Clement Adams, originated from his mission to develop trade with Moscow. Although Ivan IV initially welcomed Chancellor's trade mission, highly profitable for the English Muscovy Company, political disagreements exasperated him. The venture ended in insults to Queen Elizabeth, whom Ivan labelled "a vulgar old maid" (poshlaia devitsa). Florinsky, *Russia*, pp. 205-207, and S.F. Platonov, *Moscow and the West* (Hattiesburg: Academic International Press, 1972), pp. 6 ff.

3. Quitrent schedules (obrochnyi urok): an annual payment for lands or various other considerations, a form of taxation as well as rent.

4. Chancellery of the Royal Household (Prikaz Bol'shogo Dvortsa): the crown agency entrusted with provisioning and managing the prince's estate and residence.

5. Parish clergy (beloe dukhovenstvo): those priests of the Russian Orthodox Church who did not take monastic vows, but lived in the world and married; they were restricted to the functions of parish priests and could not rise in the church hierarchy.

6. Moscow was theorized to be the "Third Rome" by Abbot Philotheus (Filofey) of a Pskovian monastery. Rome and Byzantium had fallen through their sins, and Moscow as their successor was destined to be the one and final center of Christianity.

CHAPTER SEVEN

1. On Alexis Adashev, see Hugh F. Graham, "Adashev, Aleksei Fedorovich," MERSH, Vol. 1, pp. 28-30.

2. The Novgorod government was in many respects similar to that of a city state, with only formal vestiges of feudal rule in that a prince was "contracted" to defend the city in case of war. The great merchant city retained much independence throughout the Tatar period through paying a limited tribute. It fell to Moscow in the late fifteenth century, but continued to be an important cultural and art center.

3. The five quarters (districts) of Novgorod seem to have been established to assess taxation conveniently during the Tatar period; they included only the immediate vicinity of the city, not outlying territories. Vernadsky, *The Mongols and Russia*, pp. 231-232.

4. Catherine II, a princess of Anhalt-Zerbst in Germany, made her way to the Russian throne by disposing of her husband Peter III, the legitimate ruler. She brought European cultural currents into Russia during her long, brilliant but debauched reign (1762-1796). See David M. Griffiths, "Catherine II," MERSH, Vol. 6, pp. 118-132.

5. Joseph Sanin, abbot of the Volokolamsk monastery, supported adherence to religious rituals, strict interpretation of Orthodox dogma, and retention of secular wealth by the monasteries. He also advocated subservience to the tsar in the spirit of caesaropapism. See Soloviev, *History*, Vol. 9, pp. 148 ff.

6. Joseph's staunch opponent, Nil Sorsky (1433-1508), held that Christianity is properly expressed inwardly and in private; the ritual and pomp of the Russian Orthodox Church of his time diminished, even negated, true worship of God. In his view a monk should live ascetically and in the wilderness, studying holy scripture in order to achieve true understanding. Nil Sorsky put his beliefs into practice in the movement known as the Trans-Volga hermits. See Florinsky, *Russia*, pp. 166 ff.

CHAPTER EIGHT

1. Musketeers (streltsy): a military force, chiefly infantry, which began in the sixteenth century and grew to number perhaps 35,000, then was eliminated by Peter the Great after they revolted several times against the tsar's control.

2, Ataman or hetman: a cossack leader. Originally elected by the free cossacks, he came to be appointed as the cossacks lost their independence and fell under the tsar's control.

3. Gentry, smallholding provincial gentry (pomeshchik): the holders of very limited estates under the system of land grants for civil and military service to the crown.

CHAPTER NINE

1. The Hanseatic trade association included the city of Novgorod as an eastern terminus. Mighty cities of northern Germany such as Hamburg, Lübeck, Bremen and Cologne, and the Baltiç cities of Riga and Tallinn, participated in this merchant monopoly, enjoying tremendous economic power in the thirteenth and fourteenth centuries. See Platonov, *Moscow and the West*, pp. 4-5, and Soloviev, *History*, Vol. 9, pp. 42-43.

2. Honored merchant (gost): a prestigious merchant with special privileges granted by the crown; in return, he collected state revenues and liquor taxes.

3. Local hundred (chernaia sotnia): at this time a provincial organization of craftsmen and merchants, much like a guild. The term later was applied to reactionary supporters of the tsar, particularly during the 1905 revolution, in plural form as "Black Hundreds."

4. The Time of Troubles is the term for the tumultuous years following the death of Boris Godunov, climaxing in the election of Mikhail Romanov as tsar. Between 1605 and 1613, the imposter False Dmitry attained the throne through a combination of chicanery and clever manipulation of popular unrest. After his murder, Vasily Shuisky briefly sat on the tsar's throne, only to be deposed in his turn in 1610. Three years of chaos ensued in which a Polish prince, Wladyslaw, was placed on Russia's throne. He too was soon deposed. See S.F. Platonov, *The Time of Troubles*. Ed. and trans. by John T. Alexander. Lawrence, 1970.

5. Old dweller (starozhilets): a peasant who had resided on lands under a landowner or other administration (such as the crown) for some time, and who usually had incurred debts which bound him to his master. With the passage of time his status deteriorated in the direction of bondage until serfdom emerged in the seventeenth century. Also a local expert on land boundaries and ownership in judicial proceedings.

6. Boris Godunov, elected tsar by his fellow boyars after being chief councillor for Ivan IV's incompetent son Fedor, reigned 1598-1605. Boris's contributions to Russian history are disputed; see Florinsky, *Russia*, pp. 220-230, and Platonov, *Boris Godunov. Tsar of Russia*. Gulf Breeze: Academic International Press, 1973.

CHAPTER TEN

1. District communal authorities: Presniakov's term is *uezdnye vsesoslovnye obshchestva*.

2. See V.I. Sergeevich, *Drevnosti russkago prava* (The Antiquities of Russian Law), 3 vols. (St. Petersburg, 1908-1911), and Kliuchevsky's *Kurs russkoi istorii*.

3. Chamber of Settlement (raspravnaia palata): an institution for the discussion of legal matters at the highest level.

4. Assembly of the Land (zemski sobor): convened by the sovereign, during the sixteenth and seventeenth centuries, the Assembly brought together representatives of all segments of the population to advise the ruler on questions of national importance.

5. Dmitry Pozharsky, a prince, and a butcher from the Volga city of Nizhny Novgorod named Kuzma Minin, are credited with organizing popular Russian forces to expel the Polish Prince Wladyslaw and Marina Mniszek from Moscow in 1611-1612. See Florinsky, *Russia*, pp. 242-244, and Platonov, *The Time of Troubles.*

6. Michael Romanov, the first ruler of the Romanov dynasty, was elected by the assembly of boyars in 1613. See Florinsky, *Russia*, pp. 249 ff.

7. Oath on the cross (krestotseloval'naia zapis): a solemn promise sealed by the ritual of affirming one's word by kissing the cross when making or signing an agreement.

8. The election of Prince Wladyslaw to the Russian throne was an attempt to restore peace and order in the face of threatening Polish invasion. The consequences, however, were burgeoning civil war. See Florinsky, *Russia,* pp. 238 ff.

9. Council of all the Land (sovet vsei zemli): Presniakov uses this term synonymously with "Assembly of the Land;" it clarifies the meaning and purpose of the former term.

10. The assembly of the territorial militia of Nizhni Novgorod during the Time of Troubles.

11. The foreign candidate, Polish Prince Wladyslaw, was a Roman Catholic.

12. Patriarch Filaret was the father of Michael Romanov. Prior to Michael's election Filaret was raised to the post of metropolitan of Moscow and, upon his return from captivity in Poland, acted as the real ruler of Russia. See Florinsky, *Russia*, pp. 229-251 *passim.*

CHAPTER ELEVEN

1. On Yury Krizhanich, see Ante Kadic, "Krizhanic's Formative Years," *American Contributions to the Fifth International Congress of Slavists*, Vol. 2, pp. 167-200; "Krizhanic's Memorandum," *Jahrbücher für Geschichte Osteuropas*, Vol. XII, No. 3, pp. 331-349; and Paul N. Miliukov, *Outlines of Russian Culture*, Vol. III, Part 1: *The Origins of Ideology.* Ed. and trans. by Joseph L. Wieczynski (Gulf Breeze: Academic International Press, 1974), *passim.*

2. Krizhanich's use of "Catholic" expresses his vision of a union of the Orthodox and Catholic churches under the pope.

3. Bohdan Khmelnitsky, a leader of the Zaporozhie cossacks on the Dnieper river, led a peasant rising against Poland in 1648. See Florinsky, *Russia.* p. 260.

4. On the Nerchinsk agreement between China and Russia, see M.I. Sladkovsky, *China and Japan. Past and Present*. Ed. and trans. by Robert F. Price (Gulf Breeze: Academic International Press, 1975), p. 25. Also Ken Shen Weigh, *Russo-Chinese Diplomacy*, 1689-1924 (Bangor, 1967), pp. 3-13.

5. Afanasy L. Ordin-Nashchokin served as a close advisor to the second Romanov tsar, Alexis Mikhailovich.

6. "Circassians" (Cherkas) was the term used in the seventeenth century and earlier for the cossacks dwelling in the area north of the Black Sea.

7. Patriarch Nikon and his reforms brought a major crisis in Russian religious life. His changes in ritual and church governance marked a return to original Greek Orthodox practices as revealed by scholarly research into the original sources. These outward rituals did, of course, symbolize an innovative scholarly attitude which was repugnant to the Orthodox populace and which provoked a large and lasting dissidence. See Florinsky, *Russia*, pp. 286 ff.

8. "Old Believer" sects appeared in reaction to the innovations of Nikon. Their adherents were persecuted and forced to flee to the vast forests of Russia, where the sectarians became isolated. With the passage of time, some developed varied rites for self-humiliation and the expression of religious zeal. When persecution continued, many sectarians emigrated in the late nineteenth century to distant lands, including the United States and Canada. See Florinsky, *Russia*, pp. 293 ff.